David Leavitt

AF114680

City Document—No. 60.

REPORT

OF THE

JOINT STANDING COMMITTEE

ON

BOSTON HARBOR,

FOR THE YEAR

1852.

BOSTON:
1853.
J. H. EASTBURN, CITY PRINTER.

CITY OF BOSTON.

In Common Council, December 9, 1852.

Ordered, That the Committee on the Harbor have authority to report in print; and if they are unable to report before the close of the year, that they be authorized to transmit their report to the next Council.

HENRY J. GARDNER, *President.*

In Board of Mayor and Aldermen, December 13, 1852.

Passed in concurrence.

BENJ. SEAVER, *Mayor.*

Committee on Boston Harbor, for the year 1852.

Benjamin S. Allen,	Edward H. Eldredge,
Benjamin James,	Samuel R. Spinney,
of the Board of Mayor	David Hamblen,
and Aldermen.	*of the Common Council.*

REPORT.

The Committee appointed, in the organization of the City Council, in the year 1852, in accordance with the provisions of the City Ordinance, relating to the preservation of Boston Harbor, passed November 12, 1846, and who were authorized by an order of the Council of the 9th and 13th of December, 1852, to report in print and to transmit their report to the present Council, have attended to their duty and submit the following

REPORT:

Very soon after their appointment, the attention of the Committee was called to their duty, by the reference to them of several orders of notice upon petitions to the General Court, praying for permission to extend wharves and make other improvements in and around the harbor. With a strong desire to give the questions, thus presented to them, that careful examination which their importance demanded, the Committee encountered great difficulty from the want of accessible and authentic information. It was obviously necessary that they should understand the common law and the history of past Legislative action in regard to the subject, as well as the original conformation of the harbor, and the mode in which that had been affected by natural or artificial causes.

In considering the petitions referred to, the Committee gave hearings to several of the parties in interest, and from various other sources obtained such information as lay in their power; a great amount of conflicting testimony was thus adduced, which further impressed upon them the necessity of obtaining an accurate and reliable statement of all the facts bearing upon the subject.

To obtain these facts and to state them in a methodical form became then their primary object, and though they soon found that their term of office was likely to expire before that object could be accomplished, they were encouraged to proceed with their investigations by the hope that their labors might alleviate those of their successors, and perhaps suggest such a course of action as should perpetuate the knowledge and experience gained from year to year, in such a shape as to be of service to the City.

The Harbor of Boston extends from a cluster of islands on the east, called the Brewsters, to the head of tide water in the Charles and Mystic rivers and the South Bay. An essential difference in the two portions of the harbor and the necessity of entirely different treatment for their preservation, have led to a distinction between the outer and inner harbors; the outer harbor reaching from the ocean to a line passing through Governors' Island, north and south, and the inner harbor comprising all the tide waters to the westward of that line.

The outer harbor is protected from the encroachments of the ocean by several islands, which are indeed the chief bulwarks of the harbor; they break the sea as in violent storms it rolls furiously in from the ocean, and make comparatively still water and safe anchorage ground within. They serve, too, an important purpose in directing the tide-waters, as they ebb and flow through the main channels, thus maintaining a depth of water sufficient for the largest vessels. But exposed as they are to the full force of our easterly gales, and to constant abrasion by the sea, these islands and the external headlands of the harbor are continually wasting away. Very important changes have already taken place; islands which less than a century ago were sufficiently large to be occupied as sheep pastures, have entirely disappeared. Of Bird Island and Nix Mate, for example, nothing now remain but shoals, covered by the tide at high water. These changes, however serious in themselves, have been attended by others still more alarming; the debris thus washed away from island and headland, have in process of time formed new shoals, and in some places created bars or spits which project from the islands in dangerous proximity to the main channels.

The City Government have made great exertions in previous years to apprize Congress of these important facts, and their earnest representations have not been without effect, very considerable sums of money having been appropriated by the National Legislature, for the purpose of erecting sea walls on several of the islands to prevent the further injurious action of the sea. A statement of what has been already done by the government of the United States, will be found in another part of this report; and it will also thence appear, that although much has been done, there yet remains much to do for the protection and preservation of the outer harbor.

The deteriorating causes which act upon the inner harbor are different in their nature, and although as yet no essential injury has been produced, they are not less to be feared and guarded against. The channels of the harbor being formed and continued by the tide-waters passing to and from the great reservoirs of the Charles and Mystic Rivers and the South Bay, and the scouring or deepening effect of the tides in passing through the channels, being in proportion to the quantity and velocity of the ebb—it follows as a natural result, that any material reduction in the area of those reservoirs must necessarily reduce the quantity of water and diminish the velocity of the current, and thus injuriously affect the channels. It therefore becomes a matter of the first importance to protect these reservoirs from encroachment, and to maintain as nearly as possible their natural and ancient size or water capacity.

From the best information to be obtained it appears that the original area of the inner harbor, including channels, flats and marsh lands, covered by high tides, as specified in the report of the City Engineer, did not vary much from seven thousand two hundred and twenty-eight acres. The present area covered by high tides, as stated in the same report, is as follows, viz:—

Of Charles River, above Charles River bridge,	1,101 acres.
Of Mystic River, above Chelsea bridge,	838
Of Miller's River and Prison Bay,	219
Of South Bay above South Boston bridge,	316
Of all other waters,	3,385
In all,	5,859 acres.

Thus it appears that the original water area has been diminished one thousand three hundred and sixty-nine acres.

Of the area covered at the present time by high tides, one thousand and thirty-four acres are within the lines claimed by riparian owners, and if they held a legal title to the same, without restriction as to use, the harbor might be filled up and the tide forever excluded to that extent.

It is from the injudicious use of their property by these riparian owners, and from the improper filling up of portions of those ancient reservoirs that the principal danger to the inner harbor is to be apprehended. The reduction of the original area of the harbor already noticed, has been chiefly caused by such encroachments, the nature and extent of which and their effect upon the City and the harbor respectively, are strikingly exhibited upon a map prepared by the City Engineer, at the request of the Committee, and attached to this report.

The nature and extent of the jurisdiction of the Commonwealth over the flats in the harbor have been the subjects of very considerable discussion, and have received the attention of several boards of commissioners appointed by the General Court.

The title of the Commonwealth is founded in the first place, on the right of eminent domain, the right which every sovereign State possesses of disposing of all the property within its jurisdiction, as the safety and well being of the whole may require; but if, in the exercise of this right, private property be taken for public use, the State is bound by the Constitution to make compensation therefor.

There is also a title vested in the Commonwealth to what is termed "the soil of the sea," that is, to the land covered by tide waters within its territorial limits; being a right to the ground only, while the right of passage over it, is common to every individual in the community.

It is not proposed to consider this part of the subject in detail—the title as claimed for the State is here simply stated, and reference is made to the able exposition of the law contained in the report of the Commissioners appointed under the legislative resolve of May 3d, 1850.*

---

* See page 42 of the Appendix.

The right of building into and over the tide-water of the Commonwealth, rests upon the Old Colony law of 1641, which is the following, viz.:

"It is declared that in all creeks, coves and other places about and upon salt water, where the sea ebbs and flows, the proprietor of the land adjoining, shall have propriety to low water mark, where the sea doth not ebb above one hundred rods, and not more where it ebbs further.

"*Provided*, that such proprietor shall not by this liberty have power to stop or hinder the passage of boats or other vessels in or through any sea, creeks or coves to other men's houses or lands."

This law, as determining the extent of riparian ownership, has been variously construed, but the highest legal opinion considers the grant and proviso as equally important in defining the extent of such ownership and restricting the use of it, and a recent decision of the Supreme Court sustains the authority of the Legislature to establish harbor lines beyond which no wharf shall ever be extended into tide water.*

The legal control over the flats, marshes, and tidal ways of Boston Harbor is thus held by the Commonwealth. The policy pursued by the General Court was for many years exceedingly liberal, and had reference mainly to the requirements of a rapidly increasing business community and the pressing demand on all sides of the City for more land. The ultimate injury to the harbor, that might result from the extensive encroachments authorized by the General Court, seems for a time to have been lost sight of, or if it were considered at all, it was left to the future to protect this great interest, when protection should have become absolutely necessary.

---

* See in page 56 of the appendix, an abstract of the decision referred to, prepared by C. W Storey, Esq.

At an early day, the City authorities, as before stated, manifested great interest in this subject. They took measures to represent to the National Government the injurious effects upon the channels of the outer harbor, occasioned by the gradual washing away of the islands and headlands, and petitioned for and obtained several large appropriations for their preservation.

For the first active steps, in this, as well as in many other matters of great importance to the City, we are indebted to the Hon. Josiah Quincy, then Mayor, who, in November, 1823, called the attention of the City Council to the importance of securing Deer and Rainsford Islands from the inroads of the sea. A committee was in consequence appointed, who reported in the same month that an examination of those islands, made in company with Commodore Bainbridge and other gentlemen skilled in maritime concerns, had resulted in a conviction of the importance of taking immediate measures to secure them from the inroads of the sea. The committee recommended that a memorial should be immediately addressed to Congress, asking for an appropriation to preserve those great defences of the harbor, upon which its safety and convenience and the commercial prosperity of the City depended. They also suggested the erection of a breakwater * and the procurement of a law prohibiting the taking away of ballast from any of the islands. The report was agreed to, and a committee appointed to carry it into effect.

On the 8th of December, 1823, the mayor brought also before the City Council the importance of the immediate purchase of George's and Lovell's Islands, the former being, in the opinion of men of great nautical skill,

---

* Municipal History of Boston, page 117. For the resolutions of the City Government, see Appendix, page 72.

the bulwark of the harbor, both as being the best site for a fortress, and as affording the only secure anchorage ground in the outer harbor for vessels of every size and description, during easterly gales. He had ascertained that those islands, of such inestimable importance to the City, were the property of one individual who derived from them an income by the sale of stone and gravel, and thus assisted the inroads of the sea. By these combined operations one-half of George's Island had been destroyed, and both of the islands could then be purchased for the sum of seven thousand dollars.

The council were not, however, prepared to adopt the suggestion of the mayor, but referred the subject to their successors.

In November, 1824, the mayor again brought this subject before the City Council, stating that these islands ought to belong to the City; and that although the duty of fortifying the harbor belonged to the United States, yet a favorable opportunity for vesting the title to any of its natural defences in the city ought not to be lost. He added, that the adoption of such a measure by the City Council would strongly express their sense of the importance of those islands and exert a propitious influence in favor of any application to Congress for their protection.

This persevering urgency of Mr. Quincy effected its object. The sanction of the City Council was obtained, and a committee appointed with full powers, who reported, in March, 1825, that George's and Lovell's islands had been purchased for six thousand dollars, upon satisfactory terms and conditions.

Negotiations with the General Government were then entered into, in the course of which the views of the City Council were ably sustained by James Lloyd and Daniel Webster, then the senators of Massachusetts in Congress, and they resulted in a transfer to the United States of the soil and jurisdiction of George's Island, and so much of Deer Island as should be covered by their works, and in an appropriation by Congress of forty thousand dollars for the protection of George's and Deer islands by sea walls. This sum was, however, applied to, and exhausted in protecting George's Island only.

In November, 1827, Mr. Mayor Quincy again called the attention of the City Council to the state of the several islands and beaches in the different portions of the harbor, stating that the former appropriation made by Congress had been expended, and that additional appropriations were requisite for the protection of the harbor. At the same time, he called their attention to a petition, pending before the Legislature of the State, from the town of Chelsea, relative to the jurisdiction over Chelsea beach and to the importance of maintaining that beach in its present state. He adverted also to the practice of taking ballast and sand from Bird Island, and from the bar extending from the Great Brewster to the stone monument at the entrance of the narrows.

An application to the Legislature was accordingly authorized, and an act obtained, providing against the several injuries which were specified or apprehended.*

In 1828, a memorial to Congress, showing the importance of the protection of Deer Island, was prepared and forwarded by the City Council, and was ably sustained by Mr. Gorham, the representative of the City in the House. An appropriation of eighty-seven thousand dollars was thereupon made, for the purpose of erecting a sea-wall on Deer Island, which was commenced in the same year.

The sagacity and foresight which prompted these early movements for the preservation of the outer portion of

* Municipal History of Boston, page 119.

the harbor, and the energy and perseverance which pressed them to a successful conclusion, were, with reference to the inner harbor, further displayed in the same year (1828), when the proprietors of wharves at the northerly part of the City, petitioned the Legislature for permission to extend their wharves into the channel of the harbor.

The Mayor, apprehensive that such permission might injuriously affect the free navigation of the channel, requested the Legislature to suspend its proceedings, and by special message brought the subject before the City Council, as being obviously of great importance. After stating the probable consequences of inconsiderate action, as well in granting authority to extend wharves, as in the mode of carrying such grants into effect, he suggested that merchants and other persons acquainted with the circumstances of the harbor should be appointed commissioners to examine and report, upon every petition for leave to extend any structure into the harbor, such facts and opinions as might guide the City Government in deciding on its merits; and that every grant of such permission, made by the Legislature, should be on condition that the work should be executed in a manner satisfactory to the City Council.

This recommendation resulted, finally, in the passage of an order for the appointment of a joint committee of the two branches of the City Council, to take such measures as they might deem proper to protect the rights and interests of the City, in the extension of wharves into the channel of the harbor, with power to appear before the Committee of the Legislature that had the subject in hearing, and, if necessary, to employ the City Solicitor to maintain the rights of the City in the premises.

It will be seen that the powers given to this committee were very similar to those possessed by the present

Joint Standing Committee of the City Council, which was provided for by an ordinance passed in 1846.

In 1829 the attention of the City Council was again called to the subject, by a special message from the Mayor, Harrison Gray Otis, it having been represented that the channel, extending from Long Wharf southerly to South Boston new bridge, was becoming more shallow from various causes, that vessels lying at the wharves in that space were endangered by easterly storms; and that there was no position in that quarter, which could be safely occupied by steamboats.

It was the opinion of the Mayor, that if the flats lying east of the channel (beyond the reach of individual claims) were the property of the City, improvements might be made upon them by means of breakwaters or island wharves, that would afford effectual protection to the harbor and wharves in that quarter, and obviate the increasing shallowness of the channel; that such improvements might be made without expense to the City, and possibly upon contracts that would afford some ultimate revenue; that it would seem proper and necessary that these flats should become the property of the City, inasmuch as memorials were and would continue to be frequently presented to the Legislature for private grants and immunities, by the proprietors of wharves and estates lying in that neighborhood, of the reasonableness or injurious tendency of which, as well as the limitations and regulations, to which, if granted, they ought to be subjected, the City Government would possess the most competent means of deciding, as the premises were constantly under their observation.

Upon the recommendation of the Mayor, a committee was appointed, who, after investigating the subject, and obtaining the opinion of the Boston Marine Society,* re-

* See Appendix, page 73.

ported the following orders, which were passed June 10th, 1829.

Ordered, That the Mayor be requested to apply, in behalf of the City Government, to the Legislature, and endeavor to obtain therefrom a grant to the City of such portions of the flats lying east of the channel and extending from the free bridge north easterly towards Fore Point channel, as may be sufficient for the purpose of establishing a wharf or breakwater, to extend from the neighborhood of Boston free bridge towards said Fore Point channel, or on such parts of said flats as may hereafter be thought proper to be used for that purpose.

Ordered, that the Senators of this County, and the Representatives of the City, be, and hereby are requested to aid in obtaining a grant of the premises for the purpose aforesaid.

In accordance with these orders, a memorial was presented on behalf of the City, to the Legislature of 1830, and was by them referred to the next General Court. The same course was taken in regard to it in 1831, and no further mention of it is made in the records.

It does not appear that any definite or important action upon subjects connected with the harbor, was taken by the City Council for several years after this date.

In the meantime, in 1835, the number of petitions to the General Court, for permission to extend wharves into the harbor, yearly increasing, the attention of that body was directed to the necessity of greater caution than had been heretofore used in granting the prayers of such petitioners; the want was felt of scientific information respecting the effect of the extensive encroachments already authorized, and under authority of a resolve passed on the 5th of March in that year, to cause a survey to be taken of certain portions of the harbor, and lines to be defined beyond which no wharves shall be extended into and over the tide-water of the Commonwealth,—the first board of commissioners was appointed by the Governor.

A full account of the action of the General Court upon the subject of the harbor, from that time to 1852, will be found in the first fifty-six pages of the Appendix. Extracts from the reports are therein given, of such length as to embody the most important opinions and views of the several boards of commissioners appointed by the State Government.

The Committee have chosen this course, rather than the insertion of such a brief summary as might properly have place in their report, confident that they could in no other way so effectually show, that, whatever special views may have been entertained by the several commissioners and committees who have examined the subject, they have all been deeply impressed with its vast importance to the City, the State and the Nation. Interesting and valuable as these reports are, they are relied upon in this connection mainly to sustain the position, that, however important our harbor may be in a national point of view, as a port of entry in times of peace, contributing largely to the revenues of the government, as the spacious gateway in times of war to the homes of a rich and happy community, defended by costly fortifications and protecting the important naval station of Charlestown; and however valuable to the State, as its greatest seaport, the great centre of its flourishing business, and indeed the very life source of that mighty impulse which throbs through every town and hamlet within its borders, which improves the mill courses, employs the mechanic, gives the farmer a market at his door, and courses over iron roads northward and westward, contributing in every way to its wealth and prosperity,—however all this may be, and whatever claims we may have upon the Nation and the State for assistance in the protection and preservation of our harbor, still, inasmuch as the harbor of Boston is of vastly more comparative importance to the City itself, than it can possibly be either to the State or the Nation, in the same ratio it becomes the duty of the City to guard with watchful eye all that concerns this vital interest.

On the 28th of May, 1838, a joint special committee of the City Council was appointed to take into consideration the defenceless state of the Harbor, and the expediency of addressing a memorial to Congress on the subject, or of instructing the representative of the City in that body to use his personal exertions to procure the adoption of suitable measures in regard to it.

On the 18th day of June, the Mayor, Mr. Samuel A. Eliot, as the chairman of this committee, reported, that a sub-committee of their number had visited the works at Fort Independence and George's Island, and conferred with Col. Thayer, the superintendent, upon the subject. The committee had thus learned that while Fort Independence was so nearly completed that the harbor would soon cease to be in that absolutely defenceless condition in which it had so long remained, yet the work upon George's Island had been suspended for want of an appropriation.

The Mayor was therefore instructed by the Council, to urge upon the representative of the City in Congress the importance of obtaining a suitable appropriation to complete the defensive works in the harbor; and to communicate with such other members of Congress on the subject, as he might think proper.

It appears by the records of the General Court that in 1843, upon a petition of the City of Boston, a resolve

(Res., 1843, chap. 16) was reported and passed, requesting the Senators and Representatives of this Commonwealth in Congress to exert themselves to procure the passage of measures to prevent further injury to the islands and headlands in the harbor of Boston from the action of the sea.

At the session of Congress in the early part of the same year, the sum of $15,000 was appropriated for the protection of Lovell's Island, and this sum was expended in the erection of a sea wall upon that island.

In 1846, by a communication from R. B. Forbes, Esq., President of the Boston Marine Society, the attention of the City Council was called to the importance of taking some immediate action in reference to the preservation of the islands and headlands of the outer harbor. A report from a committee of the society, accompanying that communication, contained some interesting information in regard to the encroachments of the sea upon the islands at the entrance of the harbor, and the importance of those islands to its preservation.

Some statements were also made in this report relating to the quantity of stone and gravel annually taken from the islands and beaches, which was estimated as follows, viz:

From Point Shirley and Chelsea beach,	50,000 tons.
From Brewster Island and the Spit,	30,000
From Deer Island,	2,000
From Long Island,	20,000
From Gallop's Island,	10,000
In all,	112,000 tons,

besides a large quantity known to be taken from Point Alderton and other places, greatly to the injury of the harbor.

Annexed to the report above alluded to, was a report

made by Col. Thayer, of the U. S. Engineers to the Treasury Department.

An order was immediately passed by the City Council appointing a committee, to whom were referred the memorial of the Boston Marine Society, and the documents accompanying the same, together with the petition of William Appleton and others relating to the same subject.

This committee reported in June, 1846; they stated that in the contemplation of the subject, its importance was so deeply impressed upon their minds as to lead them to believe, that years of labor and of thought might be considered as well rewarded, if they should be the means of enlisting the hearty and effectual co-operation of the City Government, in efforts to avert the catastrophe of which they were warned, and for the apprehension of which, they felt convinced there were strong grounds. They also submitted statistics showing the increasing commerce and the growth of the City. Statistics upon these points are constantly before the City Council, and the committee do not deem it necessary to their present purpose, to present further proof of that which falls within the individual experience of, and must be apparent to, every citizen.

There is one point of comparison, however, that in this connection deserves particular attention. The Committee of 1846, stated that within the last generation, the size of vessels intended for foreign trade, sailing from this port had been doubled, and within a much shorter period those employed in the coastwise trade, had been more than doubled in size.

"Thirty years since," they say, "a vessel of 300 tons for foreign voyages was of the largest class. Those now built for this purpose are from 5 to 600 tons, and a few reach as high as 8 or 900 tons. Thus it will be perceived, that while the capacity of the vessel has increased, the depth of water in the harbor, which is to bear her and her burthen, has as constantly, though less rapidly, decreased; and the result to our beloved City, unless prevented by those to whom belong the power and the duty to do it, must be disastrous in the extreme."

Through the kindness of Gen. Andrews of the Registry Office, Boston Custom House, the Committee have obtained a tabular statement showing the increase in the number, as well as in the size of vessels registered at this office.* It appears that the average tonnage of the ships registered in 1850 was 1019 tons; in 1852, 1001 tons; and in the first nine months of 1853 the number was equal to that of any preceding *year*, and the average tonnage was 1236. Several have been built of more than 2000 tons burthen, and one is now about to be launched of 4000 tons.

This increase in the size of commercial vessels is not confined to Boston and its vicinity, but is equally observable in those built in other parts of the State, in Maine, New York and elsewhere, which have frequent occasion to use our Harbor.

An examination of the table of comparative soundings, carefully prepared by the City Engineer at the request of the Committee, and annexed to this report, shows, however, that the opinion that a material change has taken place in the depth of water in the channels of the inner harbor is not correct; but that the changes have been chiefly at the sides of the channels, reducing their area without diminishing their maximum depth.

In accordance with the recommendation of the Committee of 1846, an ordinance was passed creating the Joint Standing Committee of the City Council on the

* See Appendix, page 75.

Harbor; and their Report, with the accompanying documents, was transmitted to the Governor of the State, with a request that he would lay the same before the Legislature, for the purpose of inducing that body to make an appropriation for the purchase of one or more of the most exposed islands in the Harbor, or pass a law to prohibit the taking of ballast from any of them; or to address a memorial to the General Government upon this subject, which it was hoped would not be without its influence.

A communication from the Governor, accompanying the above-mentioned documents, was referred by the General Court to the Committee on Mercantile Affairs and Insurance, on the 19th of January, 1847.

The Joint Standing Committee of the Harbor made their first report on the 12th of February, 1847. It referred to Gallop's Island and the Great Brewster, and concluded with an order,—which was passed,—to authorize the Mayor to petition the Legislature for the passage of an Act to prohibit the taking of sand or gravel from those islands; and also for a grant of the flats in the Harbor lying between South Boston and the channel.

The petition of the Mayor, Josiah Quincy, Jr., was presented to the General Court, February 16th, 1847. Commencing with some remarks upon the value and importance of the Great Brewster and Gallop's Island, as constituting the principal barriers to the encroachments of the sea, and safeguards to the main channels of the Harbor; and upon their gradual diminution by the action of the water; the petition stated that the practice of taking ballast from those islands prevailed to a great extent, and tended in no small degree, as there was reason to believe, to their destruction, thereby putting in jeopardy the interests of all those concerned in the navigation of the Harbor; and concluded with a prayer for the passage of a law, with suitable penalties, prohibiting any person from taking ballast, sand, gravel or other soil from those islands, or from any of the beaches, spits or bars adjoining them, or in their immediate vicinity. This petition was also referred to the Committee on Mercantile Affairs and Insurance.

The proprietor of the Great Brewster Island, Lemuel Brackett, protested at length against the enactment prayed for, as tending to deprive him, without compensation, of the use of his property in the manner in which it had been used for a long series of years by him and his ancestors. His protest is found with the other papers relating to the subject among the files of the Senate.

The petition of the Mayor for a grant to the City, of the flats lying north of South Boston, within such limits and under such restrictions as might be necessary to preserve the rights of all concerned, was referred to the same Committee. An order of notice was issued upon it, and many remonstrances were presented against the granting of its prayer. Several of the remonstrances were signed by merchants, ship-owners and citizens of Boston; one by Marcus Morton, then Collector of the Port, and nine others, one by R. B. Forbes, the Chairman of the Committee of the Boston Marine Society, on Boston Harbor, and another by the Commercial Wharf Company, and sixteen other wharf corporations, or private wharf owners.

The Committee reported April 2d, 1847, on the subject of the Mayor's petition, and the report of the Committee of 1846, transmitted by the Governor, that it was inexpedient to legislate thereon, and this report was accepted by both branches of the Legislature.

In 1847, several orders were passed in the City Council, relating to the appointment of a Harbor Master, but as the duties of that officer are mainly connected with the enforcement of certain regulations respecting the anchorage of vessels, they are not important in this view of the subject, although they have doubtless conduced greatly to the safety and convenience of all persons concerned in the navigation of the Harbor.

September 18th, 1848, the Committee on the Harbor were directed to inquire what measures could be adopted to prevent the filling up of the ship channel between George's Island and the spit of the Great Brewster. It does not appear that the committee made any report upon the subject; the omission was probably owing to the late period of the session at which the order was passed, and to the fact that the season of the year was not favorable to the necessary examinations.

The Great Brewster Island was purchased by the City in 1848, for the sum of four thousand dollars, with a view to transfer it to the United States Government, and so to insure the building of a sea wall around it. The Commonwealth ceded the jurisdiction of the Island to the United States, and so much of the property in it, as might be necessary for the construction of a sea wall, was conveyed to the United States by the City.*

An appropriation of forty thousand dollars, for the construction of the wall, was made by Congress July 20th, 1848, and the work was commenced early in the next year, according to plans prepared by Col. Thayer. That accomplished officer having in charge the fortifications on George's Island, and being at that time in feeble health, he was unable to superintend the construction of the wall, and it was placed in charge of Capt. Benham, of the United States Engineers.

The sum appropriated by Congress was altogether insufficient to complete the work, and it was left when the appropriation was exhausted, or rather when $42,000 had

---

* January 30, 1849.

been expended, as it appears upon a reduced plan of the Great Brewster, showing the abrasions or waste of the island since 1820, attached to this report.

For this plan, the Committee take pleasure in acknowledging their obligations to the Hon. William Appleton, who kindly procured it for them from the Department of Engineers at Washington. An examination of the plan will show that the North Eastern bluff, now 117 feet high, has been wasted away during the last thirty years more than 150 feet; and as the slope of the bluff is towards the southwest, it is estimated that the highest point must have been at least 130 feet above high water mark. The immense body of earth which has thus disappeared, must have been deposited where it could not but prove injurious to the channels of the Harbor. It was washed from a single point by the action of the sea, and we are naturally aroused to a sense of the impending danger, when we consider the great extent of island, shore and headland at the entrance of the Harbor, constantly exposed to the same powerful and injurious agency.

The work upon the Great Brewster, though yet incomplete, has answered its purpose admirably. It is in itself a superb structure; all the principal parts of it are now as perfect as when left by the workmen, and this notwithstanding the very severe test of the great storm of April, 1851; in the course of which, however, owing to the unfinished state of the work, the sea found its way round the southeasterly end of the wall, and washed out the earth from behind to the depth of ten feet, thus exposing a portion of it on both sides of the sea.

In consequence of a communication from the Hon. William Appleton, concerning appropriations for Boston Harbor, the City Council directed the City Solicitor to prepare a Memorial on the subject, to be presented to Congress, after it should have received the sanction of the

Committee on the Harbor. The memorial was ably drawn, and met the entire approbation of the committee. In pursuance of the order of the Council, Mr. Chandler also proceeded to Washington, and took with him the Harbor Master, and Capt. Hunt, an experienced pilot, for the purpose of placing all the facts respecting the Harbor before the Committee on Commerce, to whom the Memorial was referred. On his return, the City Solicitor made a report of the result of his mission,* and the hopes then entertained, that it would be successful, proved to some extent well founded. An appropriation of $30,000 was made, on the 30th of August, 1852, for the continuation of the work at the Great Brewster Island. The representative in Congress, from this District, Mr. Appleton, made strenuous efforts to obtain an appropriation sufficient for its completion, and it is to be regretted that his efforts were not successful. The next being a long session of Congress, it is hardly probable, unless very great exertions are made, that an appropriation can be obtained in season to continue the work in the summer of 1854. It is, however, now in progress under the supervision of Col. Thayer.

It appears from a statement furnished by Gen. Totten, of the Engineer Department, that Col. Thayer's estimate for the completion of the works at this place, over and above the sum already appropriated, was $32,700, provided the work could go on continuously, excepting from the interruption of winter. If there should be another suspension of operations, the estimated cost would be magnified materially.†

On the 29th of March, 1851, a communication was addressed to the Council, by the Harbor Master, Mr. Tewksbury, representing that an immediate necessity existed for action in regard to Gallop's Island, on the pres-

---

* City Document 33—1852.   † See page 74 of the Appendix.

ervation of which depended the existence of the deep ship channel of the Narrows. This was referred to the Committee on the Harbor, and it appears by an endorsement upon it, that the City Solicitor recommended an application to the General Court on the subject. No further action was taken, however, in respect to this very important island.

It may be remarked that next in importance to the Great Brewster, for the preservation of our Harbor, are Long Island Head and Gallop's Island. Long Island Head presents to northeasterly storms a precipitous bank, rising about 100 feet above high water, and is, through the action of the sea, constantly wasting away. Fully aware of the importance of this point, and desirous of protecting it by a sea wall, Col. Thayer has several times made proposals, on behalf of the United States Government, for its purchase, but its owners profess to receive a considerable income from the sale of ballast from it, and ask for the headland a price altogether out of proportion to its value.

Gallop's Island, situated upon one side of the main ship-channel of the Narrows, although it does not present a high bank or headland to the action of the sea, is, from its immediate contiguity to the channel, of the greatest importance. The proprietor of this island has for many years been in the habit of selling large quantities of ballast, which has been taken from the island mostly between high and low water mark. Such removals of the hard surface or shingle have exposed to the action of a powerful current a part of the soil which is more easily affected by it, and a spit has consequently been formed, and is gradually making out towards the main channel from the northeasterly point of the island.* The income

---

* For a particular description of these changes, see pages 21 and 22 of the Appendix.

derived from the sale of ballast has induced the owner of this island also to place an entirely disproportionate value upon it. The language of the Supreme Court in the case of the Commonwealth vs. Tewksbury, (Suffolk March Term, 1846,) shows that such a use of the property may be prohibited by law without any improper infraction of private rights. "Without hazarding an opinion upon any other question, we think that a law prohibiting an owner from removing the soil composing a natural embankment to a valuable, navigable stream, port or harbor, is not such a taking, such an interference with the right and title of the owner, as to give him a constitutional right to compensation, and to render an act unconstitutional, which makes no such provision, but is a just restraint of an injurious use of the property, which the Legislature have authority to make."* In the opinion from which the previous extract was made, in the case of the Commonwealth vs. Tewksbury, the Court say, with reference to the Stat. 1845, c. 11, under which the defendant had been indicted for removing the soil from his own land—"The statute, though recent, is a mere revision of a former one, St. 1796, c. 73, (2 Special Laws, 283.) They are alike in substance and purpose, and the only change is, in substituting an indictment for a *qui tam* action, as the mode of prosecution. The object of both is apparent, and is a very important one, to protect the harbor of Boston, by preserving the integrity of the beaches and the natural embankments of sand and gravel by which it is bordered."†

It appears, however, that by a Statute of the succeeding

---

* 11 Metcalf Rep. 55.

† From the same opinion, we make the following quotation, which is not without interest, viz :—"The importance of such natural beaches, in a public point of view, may be estimated by the case of Plymouth Beach. The port of that ancient town was protected by a narrow strip of land, extending in front of it. In consequence of cutting away the wood upon it, or from some other cause, it was

year (Stat. 1846, c. 106,) the Statute of 1845, c. 117, was repealed as to a part of Mr. Tewksbury's beaches in Chelsea, and $500 were ordered to be paid him out of the treasury of the Commonwealth, " as an indemnity for the loss, suffered by him under the operation of said act, by reason of being unnecessarily debarred from the use of his land, for the purpose, as was intended, of securing the harbor of Boston."

The Committee are not aware of the reasons which induced such a course on the part of the Legislature of 1846, and have thought it not impossible that the fact was not brought to their notice that the law of 1845 was not new, except in the form of its sanction. It is obvious that the only way in which Mr. Tewksbury's rights were affected by that law, was that that made it the duty of the public officers to take cognizance of proceedings which had been unlawful for nearly half a century, and which had perhaps been allowed to go on with impunity, merely because the mode of punishing them was peculiarly odious.

In this connection, the committee think it not entirely useless to refer to the Act of June 12th, 1818—(Mass. Special Laws, Vol. 5, p. 254)—entitled " An Act for the preservation of Bird Island in Boston Harbor." This act provides that no earth or stones shall be taken from Bird Island without license first obtained from the Selectmen of Boston, in writing, specifying the quantity to be removed, and the object of removing it. Every person who without permission obtained as aforesaid, shall remove any earth or stones from such island, shall forfeit and pay, for each offence, the sum of twenty dollars to the use of

washed away and broken through by the wind and sea, and the navigation was in danger of being wholly destroyed. Under these circumstances, the public, the government both of the United States and of this Commonwealth, took measures, at great expense, to restore the beach, by artificial means, to its original condition."

said town. An act somewhat similar was passed, March 31st, 1834. (Mass. Special Laws, Vol. 7, Chap. 168,) entitled " An Act concerning the Islands and Beaches in the Harbor of Boston." This Act provides " that if any person shall wilfully carry away from any island in the harbor of Boston, or from any beach adjacent thereto, any earth, gravel, stone or other materials composing such island of beach, *without the consent of the owner thereof*, the person or persons so offending shall forfeit and pay for each offence, to the use of the Commonwealth, a sum not exceeding one hundred dollars nor less than five dollars," " provided that this act shall not be construed to prevent the taking of shell-fish from such islands and beaches." Section 2 of the same act imposes a like forfeiture for building a fire on Spectacle Island in the harbor, without the consent of the owner or owners thereof.

In the course of the investigations which they have found necessary for the preparation of their report, the attention of the Committee has been frequently drawn to the great extent of the researches of scientific men into the modes of preserving or improving water courses and harbors. The annals of the various scientific societies of England and the Continent of Europe are replete with valuable information derived from a vast amount of study and experiment, persevered in through long periods of years, and by the ablest engineers,—which alone could have enabled them to carry on or complete the great works now finished or in progress. Some of these works have been the means of opening to a thriving and extensive commerce, ports which were previously accessible only to the smallest vessels, or of preserving valuable harbors from impending destruction, and have thus shown that it is permitted to man, by the exercise of his intellect and the exertion of his mechanical skill, to regulate and control the wildest and most powerful agencies of physical nature. Desirous of placing before the City Council a statement of the condition of the science of Hydrography, the committee requested James Hayward, Esq. to prepare a communication on the subject, which was kindly furnished by him, and will be found in the Appendix, page 65. The attention paid by Mr. Hayward to this branch of his profession, and the great opportunities he has enjoyed of personally examining the best illustrations of it to be found in Europe and this country, render his communication highly valuable.

The Light House Board appointed by the Secretary of the Treasury under authority of the Appropriation Act of March 3d, 1851,—and which was composed of Officers of the Navy and Engineers eminent for their scientific attainments,—in their report to the Secretary, dated January 20th, 1852,—after discussing the subject of Light Houses at length, and the best modes of building and maintaining them adopted in Europe and in this country, consider the subject of buoys and the purposes for which they are intended in an elaborate and interesting manner.

The remarks of the Board upon Boston Light will be found in the Appendix, page 79.

The committee have had frequent conferences with several of the most experienced pilots in the city, and have found them uniformly disposed to afford the committee every facility, and communicate to them all the information in their power. They have received also a written communication from Mr. Gurney, which is inserted in the Appendix, page 77, and will be found interesting.

The committee having thus, in pursuance of the plan stated in the outset, presented a brief statement of all the important historical facts bearing upon the subject of the Harbor, which a careful investigation has disclosed to them; and having stated the result of examinations made under their direction, which have required no inconsiderable amount of labor and time; they here take occasion to say, that in collecting the materials for their report, they have been more and more deeply impressed with the importance of the subject, the paucity of information in regard to it, and the necessity of early and efficient action upon it, on the part of the City Council.

It is obvious from what has been said, that no actual control over the flats, water-ways or channels of the harbor is legally vested in the City of Boston. Nothing therefore can be done in the matter but through the action of the State and National Governments; except, indeed, that the City can become by purchase the owner of certain islands and headlands before mentioned as being of great value for the preservation of the harbor. Future City Councils must be the judges as to the expediency of such purchases. There is ample precedent for such expenditure; and it is to be hoped that the City Government will avail itself of favorable opportunities, which will probably occur, to obtain a title to those strong, though perishable, harbor defences. Such an ownership will not only give to the City the sole use and management of these places, but may lead to an arrangement with the United States Government, by which the system of erecting sea walls, already proved to be so beneficial, shall be continued and completed.

With regard to any action which may be had, as above suggested, through the State or National Governments, it is to be observed that the subject in contemplation is very complicated; demanding a large application of scientific principles, with an ample basis of practical observation. The committee feel assured that no man or body of men could, with the present data only, construct a plan of proceeding which should embrace all the conditions and anticipate all the difficulties of the question.

The risk of failing to achieve the best mode of remedy is involved with another even more serious,—that of making worse the present condition of the harbor. Every island and point of land,—indeed, every obstruction in the harbor, natural or artificial, communicating, through the common medium of the water, with all the others, affects and is affected by their condition, while the water reciprocally suffers a variation in all its currents by a change in any of the solids which it surrounds. Every dilapidation of an island is the beginning of a shoal, and a power added to encroachment in some new direction. These facts suggest the difficulty of the problem which is to be solved, in securing the harbor from further injurious change.

No subject can come before the City Council, upon which a greater diversity of opinion exists, or in relation to which more numerous and adverse interests are represented, than that of the changes in the inner harbor, for which petitions are presented at every meeting of the State Legislature.

Scientific men do not always agree as to the effect of contemplated changes, nor as to the influence of various methods of obtaining compensating supplies of water. Successive Boards of Commissioners, by the difference of opinion expressed in their reports, have convinced the public of the intrinsic difficulty of the subject; and from parties directly or indirectly interested in local improvements, we have every possible reason urged that the ingenuity of individual interest can suggest.

It is, however, agreed upon all hands, that Boston has no interest paramount to that of her harbor. Upon its preservation depends her commercial prosperity. If through neglect or misfortune, it shall ever become insufficient to accommodate the largest vessels employed in commerce, from that moment her decline will commence. And it will not readily be believed that a city which has always displayed so much sagacity to discern and energy to pursue her true interests, will have failed to inform herself upon a point so vital as this to her wellbeing. The best and most accurate information, and the soundest opinions respecting the harbor, will, on the contrary, always be expected of the City in her corporate capacity. Her opinion will be respected, and her influence felt in the commencement, and during the progress of any action on the part of the Governments of the State or the United States, in regard to the harbor.

The City, therefore, is bound to place herself in a position to supply the best and most comprehensive information possible with regard to the actual changes in the outer as well as the inner harbor. The formation of the Harbor Committee, a Standing Committee of the City Council, was one step towards this desirable end, but with the liability to an entire change of its members annually, and with the limited means now at their disposal, consistent progressive action on their part is extremely difficult if not impossible. It is to be considered that the experience of one Committee does not descend to their successors, and that a considerable time may be required for each successive committee to apprehend even the elements of the subject.

In entering upon the duties of their office, each committee should find in the archives of the City the means of availing themselves readily of the experience of their predecessors and seeing at a glance the existing condition of the harbor, and the nature of the changes to which it is subject, and of the plans proposed for its improvement. To obtain the knowledge required to deal properly with this question, to discover when and where proposed alterations would be injurious or beneficial, or how to frame a petition to either Government for aid, it becomes necessary to adopt a system of observation, to be continued for a series of years, and until a sufficient collection of facts shall have been made to form the basis of a correct opinion. It is only by a course of continuous observations, that we can hope to mature a system that shall effectually preserve the harbor.

The committee, therefore, respectfully recommend the immediate adoption of measures to secure a careful observation of the harbor and the changes going on within it, and an investigation of the causes of such changes, under the direction of the City Engineer, who shall be required to make an annual report thereon.

Accurate surveys of the islands and headlands should be made yearly, and the results delineated on plans drawn upon a large scale, so as to show the comparative abrasions of their soil, one season with another, and direct attention to the points most seriously affected by the action of the sea. By this means also the formation of shoals and spits, and the changes of current injurious to the main channels of the harbor, would be accurately known and defined.

Soundings should be accurately made in certain lines, at stated intervals, and their results recorded in a permanent form. It has been found that the preliminary arrangements necessary to locate these lines involve the chief part of the expense attending such examinations. Permanent monuments can be erected, which will enable the engineers to trace the most important of the lines without new instrumental observations, and the expense would then be comparatively inconsiderable.

The publication of the reports above-referred-to would inform the citizens generally upon a subject in which all are interested, and would probably exercise an influence on the public mind strong enough to overrule the efforts of private speculation, when they are opposed to the public interest.

It will be seen by reference to the resolves of the City Council, passed November 24th, 1823, (Appendix page 72,) that a very similar project was then entertained by the City Government. If the surveys then authorized had been made, and had been continued during the thirty years that have since elapsed, there would probably be now sufficient information upon the subject of harbor changes.

In the mean time, although the proprietors of certain islands may have rendered themselves liable to indictment by such use of the property as has been injurious to the public, yet as they probably proceeded under a misapprehension of their rights, and as it is desirable that all parties interested should have an opportunity to be heard in defence of their rights, the committee recommend the presentment of a petition to the General Court, setting forth the present state of facts, and praying for the enactment of a law to prohibit the owners or other persons from taking stone, sand or gravel for ballast or other purposes from any of the islands, headlands, beaches or shores, within or surrounding the harbor.

The recent examinations, made at the request of the committee, have disclosed many encroachments upon the harbor, beyond the lines established by law as the limits of any structure whatever. This indicates an urgent demand for permanent, visible monuments defining the limits alluded to. Any future encroachments would thus be matters of entire publicity, and trespassers would be at once detected, if the law and a sense of right were not sufficient to prevent any attempt to invade the public interests.

A request for an appropriation, to defray the expense of establishing such monuments, might well be included in the before-mentioned petition for a protective law.

The Attorney of the Commonwealth, for this District, has been directed to prosecute all cases of encroachment under the acts establishing the lines of the harbor. But to enable him to do this, those cases must be brought to his notice. On the 16th of April, 1846,* a commission was appointed to report the facts in all cases of violation of these acts, but such a mode of proceeding necessarily causes delay; and the committee would recommend that the City Solicitor be directed to take the proper measures to set on foot prosecutions against those who have, as appears by the statement of the City Engineer, encroached upon the harbor lines.

Besides the encroachments upon the waters of the Harbor, caused by the extension of wharves beyond the Commissioners' lines, it will be seen by the report of the City Engineer, that in several instances at East Boston it has been found that proprietors have extended the solid structure of their wharves beyond the limits authorized by the most liberal construction of the law.

In all acts granting permission for such extensions, the following clause has been inserted, viz: "provided, also, that so much of said wharf as may be constructed below said low water mark shall be built on piles, which piles shall not be nearer to each other than six feet in the direction of the stream, and eight feet in a tranverse direction."

It is evident that solid structures must have a more powerful effect in changing the direction of the channels than wharves upon piles, and if the judicious restrictions of the acts have not been complied with, the parties transgressing must of course be viewed as trespassers, and

* See Appendix, page 15.

if properly presented, would no doubt be prosecuted by the District Attorney.

It appears, by the map accompanying this report, that the harbor lines are still incomplete. The petition to the General Court, before-mentioned, should contain a prayer for the establishment of such lines around the South Bay and in Mystic River, as may, upon examination, be found necessary to preserve the water capacity of those reservoirs. And it should be urged upon the Legislature, that all future grants for improvements in the harbor should be made upon the express condition, that the compensating supplies of water, so essential to the continuance and preservation of the channels, shall be adequately provided by the grantees, under the direction of one or more public officers.

The committee further recommend that a memorial to the General Government be prepared, stating the urgent necessity of an appropriation for the completion of the sea wall around the Great Brewster Island, and for the erection of a similar wall to protect Long Island Head.

The Committee cannot close this report without expressing their obligations to Col. Thayer for the facilities given by him for an examination of the present state of the government works in the harbor, and for valuable information upon the subject generally. They have also been much indebted to James Hayward, Esq. and to E. S. Chesbrough, Esq., City Engineer, for valuable scientific information; and to C. W. Story, Esq., for efficient aid in the collection of legislative and legal authorities.

All of which is respectfully submitted.

For the Committee,

E. H. ELDREDGE.

REPORT OF THE CITY ENGINEER.

BOSTON, JULY 8, 1852.

E. S. CHESBROUGH, ESQ.,
   City Engineer:

 Dear Sir,—I am authorized by the Standing Committee on the Harbor to request you to prepare, for the use of the City Council, a plan showing all the Commissioners' Lines established by Legislative enactment in and above the Inner Harbor of Boston, with the present limits and boundaries of wharves and other improvements encroaching upon the waters of the Harbor; to report the nature of the structures, together with such other scientific information as you may be able to collect, in reference to the effect of said improvements upon the currents and channels of the harbor; and to cause soundings to be made, which shall show the depth of water at low tide in the most important parts of the harbor.

 Also to report to the Committee a proper system of fixed boundaries or monuments, by which the Commisioners' lines may be easily ascertained and defined beyond any probable contingency.

   Very respectfully yours, &c.
       E. H. ELDREDGE.

City Engineer's Office,
Boston, *August* 13*th*, 1853.

Sir,—In accordance with your instructions of July 8, 1852, the accompanying map of the Harbor, plan of the Great Brewster, and sections of soundings, have been prepared.

In consequence of the large amount of other work called for by the city, it was impossible to make the necessary examinations and present the map and plans at an earlier day; it having been understood, from the commencement, that the amount appropriated for the purpose would not justify the employment of a large or expensive extra force.

The Harbor Commissioners' lines have been laid down on the map according to the description of them in the city ordinances. It will be seen by referring to the ordinances, that these lines have been established by different commissions, and at different times, and that they are still incomplete, especially around the southern portion of the South Bay and in the Mystic River.

The letters at the principal angular points on the Harbor Commissioners' lines, laid down on the plan, indicate the names of wharves and other localities where the angular points are, as will be seen by the table of references; and the dates show the years in which the lines were established by legislative authority, as will be seen by referring to the city ordinances, except for the lines on the Charlestown side of Mystic River, and for those on the South Boston flats towards the main channel, which have been established since the publication of the city ordinances.

In the preparation of the map, advantage has been taken of every known reliable source of information, but the principal basis has been the United States Coast Survey. As this, however, was made six years ago, it did not include many improvements and changes made since. Many of these have been obtained from the plan of the East Boston Company's lands, and from the plans of individuals and corporations, kindly loaned for the purpose. In some instances it has been necessary to re-survey wharves that have recently been altered, particularly between the Battery wharf and Gray's wharf at the North End, between Wales's wharf and the Old South Boston Bridge on Fore Point Channel, and between Craigie's and the Cambridge Bridges on the west side of the city. The intention has been to show all the wharves and other structures on the harbor as they exist at the present time, and it is believed that this object has been very nearly if not fully attained, at least as far as it could have been done without making expenditures not justified by the appropriation.

The following encroachments upon the harbor have been made beyond the Commissioners' lines:—

Amory's Wharf. Face is 4½ feet outside the line. It was supposed to be pressed out by the filling, and therefore not insisted on as an encroachment. Mentioned in report on encroachments by Messrs. Bell and Lincoln in 1847.

Tileston's, Prentice's, Liverpool and Packard's Wharves, and Pearson's Dry Dock, reported by Messrs. Bell and Lincoln as over the Line in 1847, are within the new line established in 1850.

Burchsted & Leavitt's Dry Dock (next north of Otis's wharf). Both Piers are 8½ feet over.

Foster's North Wharf. Face is 2 feet over.

Battery Wharf. North corner of projecting part of face

is 11½ feet over. South corner of do. is 7¼ feet over. Resting on piles. Extended in 1849.

North Battery Wharf. Face is parallel to line and 11 feet over. Extended in 1849. On piles.

Constitution Wharf. North corner of face is 19 feet over. The angle in the face is 24 feet over. South corner is 11½ feet over. On piles. Extended in 1837.

Aspinwall's Spar Yard (next south of Chelsea Ferry Slip). North end is 7 feet over. Angle in face is 12 feet over. South end is 13 feet over. Rests on piles. Extended in 1837.

Harris's South Wharf (next north of Chelsea Ferry). Northeast corner is 6 feet over. Southeast corner is 7½ feet over. On piles. Extended in 1849.

Richards's Wharf (now Harris's north wharf). Northwest corner is 7 feet out. Southeast corner 3 feet out. At 8 feet from the southeast corner the angle of the Commissioners' lines is on the face. On piles. Extended in 1849.

Fiske's Wharf. Face is parallel to line and 6 feet over. Extended in 1837. On piles.

Comey's Wharf. Northwest corner is 3 feet over. Southeast corner is 2 feet over. On piles. Extended in 1833 and '34.

Bartlett's South Wharf (adjoining Gray's) is 7 feet over. On piles. Mentioned by Messrs. Bell and Lincoln. Extended about 1840.

Bartlett's North Wharf (Davis's wharf). North corner is 25 feet over. South corner 16 feet over. On piles. Extended about 1840. Mentioned by Messrs. Bell and Lincoln.

Ingersoll's Wharf (between Vinal's and Chamberlin's). On piles. 8 feet over. Mentioned by Messrs. Bell and Lincoln. Extended in 1837.

Spaulding's Wharf (at foot of Poplar street). Solid structure. North corner is 12 feet over; the south corner is 15 feet over. Already a subject of litigation.

Taylor's Wharf (at foot of Poplar street). Solid structure. North corner is 40 feet over; the south corner is 27 feet over. Already a subject of litigation.

Hoppin's Wharf (at the Eye and Ear Infirmary, Charles street). North corner is 5 feet over; south corner is 4½ feet over. Solid. Extended in 1848 and '49.

What effect, if any, these structures have had in changing the direction of currents and altering the shape of the channels, beyond what would have taken place if there had been a strict adherence to the laws relating to the Harbor Commissioners' lines, it is impossible to determine; but there is reason to believe that up to this time they have not caused much injury to the harbor. This should not, however, be considered as any excuse for unlawful encroachments.

At East Boston, Kelly & Holmes's wharf extends about 16 feet, and Cunningham's wharf about 2 feet, on piles, beyond the Harbor Commissioners' lines.

The case of Alger's wharf and the Boston wharf, at South Boston, are already known as having been the subjects of judicial and legislative proceedings.

At East Boston, Jones's, Clifton's, Weeks's, Cunningham's, Tufts's, the East Boston, the Atlantic Steamship Co.'s, and the Grand Junction Railroad wharves have been extended by special acts of the Legislature, which provide that no solid structures shall be built "below low water mark." If the low water level adopted on the United States Coast Survey, which is that of the lowest spring tides observed, or 16.8 feet below the coping of the Dry Dock at Charlestown, be considered as the one intended by the Legislature, and if the chart of the

Harbor prepared for the Legislature in 1837, by Messrs. Baldwin, Thayer and Hayward, which is the best known authority on the subject, be adopted as settling where the 16.8 feet line should be, then the solid portions of the above mentioned wharves have been extended considerably beyond their lawful limits; in some instances as much as two hundred feet. If *mean* low water level, as determined by the Coast Survey, or 15 feet below the coping of the Charlestown Dry Dock, be considered as the limit intended by the Legislature, then some of these solid structures extend as much as three hundred and fifty feet beyond their lawful limits.

The lines of 16.8 and 15 feet below the coping of the Charlestown Dry Dock, and the solid portions of the wharves, in front of East Boston, will be found indicated on the map. How great the influence of these encroachments upon the currents of the harbor has been, it is impossible to determine; but that it has been considerable is very probable. No structures that have been erected during the last fifteen years have had so great an effect in changing the direction of the current of the main channel, as the East Boston wharves have had. It is a source of much regret that the Harbor Commissioners' lines could not have been established nearer the shore, around the point at the west end of Sumner street, than they now are.

It is also greatly to be regretted that the Legislature did not establish the line of low water mark by reference to fixed monuments, as the level intended cannot be determined by any of the acts referred to; and if it could be, there would be, in most cases, some difficulty in applying it; for a point below low water mark this year may, owing to changes that are constantly taking place in the harbor, be above it the next, and *vice versa*.

There is reason to believe that encroachments with solid structures, unlawfully extended below low water mark, are not confined to East Boston, but may be found around the northern and western part of the city proper; and the City's own wharf, near the Charles River Bridge, is probably no exception. The means of determining the original line of low water mark around the city proper, however, are not so satisfactory as in the case of East Boston, as no authentic record of soundings made around the city proper, previous to the building of most of the existing wharves, is to be found.

Soundings have been made on a number of lines in various parts of the harbor. As any attempt to mark their depths on the map, so as to compare them with the depths of previous soundings, would cause confusion, the lines alone have been indicated on the map, while the soundings have been marked on the sheet of sections, together with those previously made. By examining them carefully, it will be seen that since 1835, as far as examinations have been made, no perceptible diminution in the depth of the centre of the main channel has taken place, and none of importance in that of the Fore Point channel.

The sides of the channels, however, have changed in several places, being generally more shallow at the ends of the wharves than formerly; the principal exception being along the narrowest part of the channel between Boston and East Boston, where there is greater depth. From two to six feet of deposit has been made at the ends of the wharves on Fore Point channel, and it is well known that considerable expense is incurred below the Ferry wharf, on the East Boston side, in maintaining a sufficient depth of water.

The greatest observed change in any part of the harbor is that at the head of Governor's Island. As compared with the soundings of 1847, those of 1842 show a deposit there of at least 8 feet for a quarter of a mile. This appeared so astonishing, that some error in the last soundings was suspected, but other soundings, made this year, by a different assistant, on a line crossing the others, confirm those of 1852. (See Sections U and V).

So remarkable a change in less than six years appears totally unaccountable, and it is very probable that some undiscovered error will yet explain it.

The shallowest part of the main channel, as indicated on the Map of the Coast Survey, is just above the Upper Middle. (See Section U). An examination of this will show that no diminution in the depth of the centre of the channel has taken place since 1847; the section referred to makes it a little greater, but there has probably been no change. The apparent difference on this, as well as on the other sections, is owing to the difficulty there was in making the soundings to within a foot, and in taking them at points identical with those of 1847.

The bottom at this most important part of the main channel being gravelly, and so hard that an iron rod could not be made to penetrate it more than an inch or two, shows that there can scarcely be any doubt that the water is quite as deep there now as it has ever been since the first vessel sailed into the harbor.

It is very evident, however, that the width of the main channel is less than it was formerly, as extensive deposits are made on its sides, where the current is much less rapid than in its centre. The comparisons made by Lt. Davis, in his memoir to the Academy of Arts and Sciences, April 1st, 1851, between the soundings of 1817 by Com. Wadsworth, and those of the Coast Survey of 1847, make this very clear.

The flats are not only extending out, generally, but they are rising higher from the accumulated deposits upon them. It is not easy to determine the rate at which they rise, if there is a uniform one; but a comparison of Des Barres' chart with the most recent soundings shows that a considerable portion of the South Boston flats has risen from four to six feet since 1764. An examination of section A shows that the Charles River flats, near the West Boston Bridge, have risen one foot since 1835.

With regard to a system of fixed boundaries or monuments, by which to ascertain and define the Harbor Commissioners' lines, the best plan would be to survey with care the wharves which are on the angular points of the Commissioners' lines, around the city proper, on the southerly side of Charlestown, and on the westerly side of South Boston. In almost every case there are houses and streets that could be made to serve as fixed monuments of reference. All around East Boston the Harbor Commissioners' lines are so carefully described and defined with reference to streets and established lines of lots, that it will always be possible to re-establish them, if every wharf in that part of the City should be destroyed. The several surveys that have already been made, by the different Boards of Harbor Commissioners, by the United States officers, and by the City of Boston, are sufficient to show approximately where the harbor lines have been located by the Legislature; but in some cases it would be difficult to detect a variation of ten feet, owing to the uncertainty of dimensions obtained by scale from plans. Visible monuments on the wharves would be of great service, in assisting those who may make examinations to detect encroachments that might otherwise pass unnoticed.

By your verbal directions the original high water line has been traced on the map, as accurately as the sources of information obtainable at this office would allow. Much labor and research were expended, in order to make this part of the map perfect; but it is greatly to be regretted that the authorities relied upon do not agree very closely among themselves. The greatest cause of doubt is owing to the flatness of the original margin of a great part of the City, in consequence of which the differences between the line to which ordinary high water and that to which very high water flowed must have been considerable, in some places probably three or four hundred feet. This was particularly the case at the foot of the Common. The sources relied upon are the plans found in Snow's History, and Frothingham's Siege of Boston, besides those of Osgood Carleton and S. P. Fuller. E. S. Rand, Esq., has also furnished some valuable information, relative to the original high water line in the western part of the City, obtained during his examination of titles to estates there.

As this is a subject of general interest in a historical point of view, would it not be advisable to induce private individuals, who may have old plans or deeds, or any other kind of information, that would aid in correcting this portion of the map, to give or loan them to the city?

An examination of the original high water line, as laid down on the map, will give a very satisfactory view of the diminution of water area that has taken place in the harbor since the first settlement of the city. The following approximate estimates of original and present areas have been prepared to show this diminution.

Water area of Boston Inner Harbor, included between the north side of South Boston and the parallel of 40° 20′ ; *the meridian marked* 0° 3′ *east of the State House ; the shores of East Boston and Chelsea, and the bridge between them ; with the bays and inlets west of these lines ; calculated from measurements by scale from larger plans.*

Water area of Ancient Harbor as above
    defined, - - - - -   7,228 acres.

Area of filling and wharves in Boston, 493 acres.
" " " " S. Boston, 59 "
" " " " E. Boston, 99 "
" " " " Charlestown, 67 "
" " " " E. Cambridge, 46 "
Boston Water Power Company's Empty
and Full Basins, - - 591 "
Mill Dam, - - - - - 14 "   1,369 acres.

Present Water Area of Inner Harbor,   5,859 "

Area within the Commissioners' Lines
liable to be filled, on S. Boston Flats, 533 acres.
" " in South Bay, 66 "
  between Mill Dam and
  the Commissioners' Lines, 27 "
" " on West Boston Shore, 15 "
" " on Cambridge Shore of
  Charles River, 280 "
" " E. Cambridge, in Miller's River, 28 "
" " East Boston Shore, 153 "
" " Chelsea, 35 " 1137 acres.

Area of Boston Inner Harbor outside the
Commissioners' Lines, as far as established, - - - - - - 4722 "

The area of Mystic River above Chelsea
Bridge is - - - - - 838 acres.
" " Charles River above
  Charles River Bridge, 1101 "
" " Miller's River & Prison
  Bay, 219 "
" " South Bay above South
" " Boston Bridge, 316 "
" " all other waters, 3385 " 5859 "

The accompanying plan of the Great Brewster shows a most remarkable change in a short time in that part of the Harbor, and proves that without the protection the General Government is now giving to that Island, by sea walls, it would be entirely washed away in a few years. Col. Thayer of the United States' Engineers, who has charge of all the government works in the Harbor, and who has been most kind and courteous towards those who have visited or sought information relative to them, states that the location of portions of the wall laid down on the plan, but not actually built, will be changed somewhat. As the copies of the plan were all struck off before this fact was known, it was not thought necessary to have new ones printed; as the main object of the plan was to show the great exposure of that part of the Harbor, to rapid and important changes.

It may be expected, perhaps, that some suggestions will be made here relative to the future extension and alteration of the Commissioners' lines, and other matters bearing upon the preservation and improvement of the Harbor. These subjects were not embraced in your instructions, moreover they demand the close investigation of commissioners or other competent persons especially appointed for the purpose, with ample time and means at their disposal.* A very large amount of such information, of a very interesting nature, has already been embodied in the appendix to your Report.

The importance of the Harbor to the commercial prosperity of the City suggests the necessity of watching with constant care the changes that take place in it, from time to time, from whatever cause. For these changes can only be detected by examination of the parts of the Harbor affected. By comparing the results

---

* See note, page 51.

of such examinations with others obtained previously, information of great importance will be gained, and future changes and extensions of the Commissioners' lines may be made with much greater safety.

I have been principally assisted in the examinations made, and plans prepared, last year and this, by Messrs. Joseph Bennett, S. S. Greele, and W. H. Bradley, and have received much aid from Mr. George P. Tewksbury, late Harbor Master, who has pointed out the rock north east of the Great Brewster, and mentions that there are other dangerous rocks not to be found on any chart of the Harbor, but known to the pilots.

I would also acknowledge my indebtedness or valuable information to James Hayward, Simeon Borden, R. H. Eddy, William P. Parrott, and T. & J. Doane, Esqs.; and to Col. Ezra Lincoln, for so long a use of the perfect and beautiful chart of the Harbor, prepared for the State of Massachusetts under the direction of the Superintendent of the United States Coast Survey. I have also been freely allowed to borrow or copy plans and charts in the custody of the Librarians of the State Library, the Boston Athenæum, and the Massachusetts Historical Society. The copies thus obtained will be valuable for future reference.

Annexed will be found a table of reference for explaining the letters and figures on the map.

Which is respectfully submitted.

E. S. CHESBROUGH,

City Engineer.

To E. H. ELDREDGE, ESQ.,
Of the Harbor Committee of 1852.

NOTE.

Since the foregoing report went to press an important fact has been learned with regard to the Harbor of Glasgow, from the Civil Engineer and Architect's Journal for October, 1853, page 373. In a very interesting article upon the Conservation and Improvement of Tidal Rivers, by Edward Killwick Calver, R. N., Admiralty Surveyor, occurs the following: "Even in the Clyde, where vessels have been got up to Glasgow, the lower river has suffered. In 1768, where there was 12 feet at low water, the general depth is from 9 to 10 feet, and in several places it is reduced to 6 feet, or one half the original quantity." The object of calling attention to this fact is to show the impropriety and danger of adopting plans for extensive changes and improvements in the Harbor, without first investigating most thoroughly everything bearing upon, or that would be affected by, them. The great increase in the depth of water at Glasgow and the consequent benefit to its commerce by the improvements which are described by Mr. Hayward in his letter—(see Appendix page 67)—and which Mr. Calver considers the cause of the reduction of depth he mentions, has been looked upon as one of the greatest triumphs of modern engineering. The Clyde, it may be said, is different from the Harbor of Boston; but other cases different from these, and differing from each other, in a greater or less degree, will be found mentioned by Mr. Calver, and in the voluminous reports on Harbors by Committees of the British Parliament.

This opportunity is taken to acknowledge the receipt of valuable information from Capt. E. Barker, and Mr. Billings, Civil Engineer at the Navy Yard, relative to the original high water line around Charlestown. Also to say that the solid portion of Jones's Wharf which is said, on page 42, to extend beyond low water mark, *does not* encroach beyond its lawful limits.

E. S. C.

Nov. 19, 1853.

Table of Reference for the letters marking the Harbor Commissioners' Lines.

[The numbers of the pages refer to the City Ordinances published in 1850, unless otherwise mentioned.]

A	Point on the westerly side of channel of Roxbury Creek, 1000 feet from Harrison Avenue, opposite South Burying Ground,	165
B	Point 1250 feet from South Boston Bridge,	
C	Heath's Wharf, afterwards Miller's, now Evans & Miller's,	158 & 165
D	Wright's Wharf, afterwards the first wharf of the South Cove Co.,	158
E	Brown's Wharf,	156
F	Wright's North East Wharf,	156
G	Wales's Wharf,	156
H	Arch Wharf,	156
I	Otis's Wharf,	156
K	Foster's South Wharf,	156
L	Rowe's Wharf,	156
M	Long Wharf,	156
N	Union Wharf,	156
O	Battery Wharf,	156
P	Constitution Wharf,	156
Q	Richards's Wharf,	156
R	Gray's Wharf,	157
S	Vinal's Wharf,	157
T	Brown's Wharf,	157
U	Trull's Wharf,	157
V	South abutment of Warren Bridge,	157
W	Northern angle of solid part of Boston and Lowell R. R. grounds,	159
X	Northeast side of Lowell R. R. Bridge,	159
Y	West side of Cragie's Bridge,	160
Z	Northeast corner of wharf of Charles River Wharf Co.,	160
A^4	Ledge at Taylor's Wharf,	160

B^4 Southwest corner of Pier Wharf, on south side of Cambridge Bridge, - - - - - 160, 163 & 170
C^4 Point 1086 feet from northeast corner of Beacon and Charles Streets, - - - - - 164 & 170
D^4 Point at west end of Mill Dam and 20 feet from it, 164 & 170

East Boston.

A^2 Point A in south line of Sumner Street, 800 feet from Jeffries street, - - - - - - - 161
B^2 Point B in division line of upland lots, 60 and 61, - 161
C^2 " C " " " " water lots of Dunbar and Fettyplace & Samson, - - - - - - 162
D^2 Point D in range of easterly boundary line of Eastern R. R. Company's water lot, - - - - 162
E^2 Point E, 510 feet from point F, - - - - 162
F^2 " G in division line of water lots of Aspinwall and Pratt & Cushing, - - - - - - 162
G^2 Point H in range of northeast side of Maverick street, 162
H^2 " I, - - - - - - - - 162
I^2 " K of page 162 and point A of page 167, - -
K^2 " B, - - - - - - - 167
L^2 " C, - - - - - - - 167
M^2 " D, - - - - - - - 167
N^2 " E, - - - - - - - 167
O^2 " F, northwest corner of west pier of Glendon Rolling Mills, - - - - - - - - 167
P^2 Point G, east pier of Glendon Company, - - - 168
Q^2 " H, - - - - - - - - 168
R^2 " I, - - - - - - - - 168
S^2 " K, - - - - - - - - 168

Chelsea Shore of Chelsea Creek.

T^2 Point L, 202 feet from Marginal Street on west side of bridge, - - - - - - - - 168
U^2 Point M, - - - - - - - - 168
V^2 " N, - - - - - - - - 168
W^2 " O, - - - - - - - - 168
X^2 " P, southwest corner of Glendon Mills Pier, - 169
Y^2 " Q, - - - - - - - - 169
Z^2 " R, - - - - - - - - 169

A^5	Point S, southeast corner of Winnisimmet Co.'s Wharf,	169
B^5	" T, southeast corner of small pier,	169
C^5	" V, end of piling of ferry pier,	170
D^5	" W, dolphin in marsh,	170

North side of Charles River and in Millers River.

A^3	South corner of island, built by Maine R. R.,	164
B^3	South corner of northwest abutment of Cragie's Bridge.	
C^3	Point 2000 feet north from Harbor line heretofore established along the Mill Dam.	
D^3	Point on north shore of Charles River, near its mouth.	
E^3	End of 4th line on north side of old channel.	
F^3	Westerly projection of State Prison Yard; end of 5th line,	165
G^3 H^3	is 6th line.	
H^3 I^3	is 7th line. I is at Prison Point Bridge.	
I^3 K^3	is 8th line.	
K^3 L^3	is 9th line. L is abutment of Lowell R. R.,	
M^3	Westerly Wharf of Navy Yard,	160
N^3	A pier of Charles River Bridge,	160
O^3	Thompson's Wharf,	161
P^3	Southeast corner of wharf of Charlestown Land and Wharf Company,	161
Q^3	Point in range with east side of 5th Street,	161
R^3	Wharf B,	161

South Boston.

A^1	Southerly extremity of Tenth line, - - -	165
B^1	Point on northerly side of S. B. old bridge, 117 feet eastwardly from west side of the draw, - - -	159
C^1	Northerly corner of Alger's old Wharf, - - -	159
D^1	Northwest corner of George C. Thatcher's small Wharf, (64 feet from Free Bridge,) - - - -	159
E^1	Point 520 feet eastwardly from east side of Free Bridge,	159
F^1	Northwesterly limit of solid fillings, - - -	*159
G^1	Northwesterly limit of any structure, - - -	*159
H^1	Point in east line of P Street, extended northward 2800 feet from Fourth Street, - - - - -	*
I^1	Northerly extremity of a line parallel with and distant from P Street, 1400 feet, - - - - -	*
K^1	Point in northerly line of Fourth Street, 1400 feet from P Street, - - - - - - -	*
L^1	Point in east line of P street, extended northwardly 2400 feet from Fourth Street, - - - -	*
M^1	Northerly extremity of a line parallel with and distant from P Street 1000 feet, - - - - -	*
N^1	Point in northerly line of Fourth Street extended, 1000 feet from P street, - - - - - -	*

* See Acts and Resolves, 1853, Chap. 385, Sec. 2.

For lines in Mystic River, see Acts and Resolves, 1852, Chap. 105.

Encroachments.

In consequence of a mistake as to the position of the south abutment of Warren Bridge, referred to in the act of 1837, (See City Ordinances, pages 157 and 159,) several important encroachments—especially those by the Fitchburg and the Boston and Maine Railroads and Bartlett's wharves,—which should have been described in the report, were omitted. The Commissioners' lines on the accompanying map have been corrected.

APPENDIX.

APPENDIX.

The first Board of Commissioners for the survey of Boston Harbor was appointed by Governor Davis, under authority of a resolve of the Legislature, passed March 5, 1835.

" To cause a survey to be taken of such portions of the Harbor of Boston as are comprised between Boston South Bridge and the dam of the Boston and Roxbury Mill Corporation, including the wharves and flats of East Boston and of Charlestown, and to define upon a plan or plans, such lines as they shall think it expedient to establish, beyond which no wharves shall be extended into and over the tide-water of the Commonwealth, on either side of said harbor, and report their doings to the Governor and Council."[*]

This Board consisted of Messrs. Loammi Baldwin, S. Thayer, and James Hayward, all engineers of eminent scientific attainments. The Report, submitted by them January 30, 1837, is distinguished by the minuteness and accuracy of the survey, soundings and other scientific details.

Several lines were recommended by the Commissioners; they say, in reference to them, —

" They intend only to mark on one side, the extent to which wharves, either solid or on piles, may be built into and over the tide-water from the shore. But they do not decide, in any case whatever, the relative rights of individuals within it, or give by the survey and plans the boundary or breadth of any wharf or other property situated between it and the shore. We leave all legal rights as we found them, only prescribing limits we think it expedient to establish, beyond which they cannot go further into the channel or tide-water, for the general good and preservation of the harbor."

[*] By Res. 1835, Ch. 85, (April 6th,) $5,000 were appropriated to carry out the provisions of the Resolve of March 5th.
By Res. 1836, Ch. 62, (April 9th,) the Commissioners were directed to delineate the flats on maps, and give the names of the owners.
By Res. 1836, Ch. 98, (April 16th,) the Attorney General was directed to enforce the law respecting obstructions of the harbor.

South Bay, in its connection with Four Point Channel, is thus spoken of : —

" If, by any process, this great reservoir becomes contracted to any considerable extent by wharves, filling, or other construction, the channel will soon feel the injurious consequences. In fixing the lines on either side between the two bridges, we were confined by the wharves already built, or by those now building by the South Cove Company. But the channel here is principally preserved by giving such direction and position to the lines as to limit all dangerous encroachments on the scouring effect of ebb tide. Great obstructions to the passing and repassing of the tide is caused by the piles of the Free bridge, by the planked sides of the wharves above and below the draw, and by the oblique position of the bridge with regard to the current. From the south abutment of the bridge we have, upon careful examination, placed the line as before described, on the south and southeast side of Four Point channel, and if the flats here are filled up above high water in the direction marked on the plan, from South Boston, the flood tides from toward Four Point corner, nearly opposite India Wharf, will all be forced into the channel, and the ebb tides returning must take the same course, and act as a scouring current to wash out the channel and preserve its depth."

The following extracts will show their views upon a point of great interest : —

" Boston harbor being only a channel for the tide to flow in and out of the great reservoirs before mentioned, it may not be irrelevant to show how it may be suddenly or gradually destroyed, and become only a safe anchorage for the lightest coasting craft, where the largest merchant vessels and even ships of the line now ride in deep water with perfect safety. It is obvious to every reflecting man, for instance, that if a dam were to be built on the site where South Boston Free bridge, or South Boston bridge, now stands, and the tide prevented from flowing above, Four Point channel would soon be filled with sediment, and not be distinguishable from the surface of flats on the southeast side. Similar effects would also result from the erection of dams in place of Chelsea and Charles River bridge. These would stop the tides, and as there would be no current either way, silt and sediment would, in a short time, fill this beautiful part of the harbor, and render it only accessible for fishing boats.

" The Commissioners are aware that this is putting a strong case, as no such dams can ever be erected without the sanction of the Legislature. But what would evidently be the consequence in the course of a very few years by the supposed dams, will as certainly be effected more gradually, and the ruin of the harbor as complete at a more distant period, by cutting off large portions of the Charles or Mystic rivers above the two bridges, either to stop the tide altogether, or partially, from flowing and filling the extensive basins of either. When the Boston and Roxbury Mill Corporation was chartered, June 14, 1814, it was authorized also to build a dam from Boston to South Boston, not northerly or easterly of South Boston bridge. This would have cut off all South bay, probably amounting to 200 or 300 acres, and the effect would have been very injurious, if not destructive, to Four Point channel. Besides the Boston and Roxbury Mill Corporation, which, by their dam, cut off from Cambridge bay 700 or 800 acres, another dam was authorized much earlier, June 1806, from Prison point, in Charlestown, to Lechmere's point, in Cambridge, by an act establishing the Proprietors of Prison Point Dam Corporation. Instead of the dam a bridge has been substituted. This would have cut off Miller's rivers, and several hundred acres more from the great basin of Charles river."

After stating the Old Colony Law of 1641, they add —

"This is all the written law we have upon the subject, upon which many principles at common law and points of practice have been decided in the courts, with which the commissioners have no concern."

"But they believe, and feel it to be their duty to state the reasons, that the full and equal enjoyment of rights given by this ancient law is inconsistent with the existence of the harbor. An instance is presented in South bay. The proprietors of the shores surrounding the flats of this basin have a right to build their wharves or solid filling, extending one hundred rods into and over the tide-water, if not interrupted by channels within that distance. As we do not know any legal objection to their exercising or selling this right, and one hundred rods in width round the said basin will make a considerable part of its area, Four Point channel may be effected, and as South Cove Company has already filled nearly all the surface of flats between the two bridges, by an act of January 31, 1833, the absolute ruin of that channel hangs upon the contingency whether the ancient law is in force relative to the tide-water of South bay, and whether the owners will ever exercise their rights. The same effects may be produced in numerous places on the Charles and Mystic rivers, by a different mode, but quite as fatal to that part of the harbor."

By an Act of the Legislature, passed April 19, 1837, the line was established, which is described in the Ordinances of the City, pages 156 and 157, and shown upon the plan attached to this report, as one of the lines in Boston Harbor, beyond which no wharf or pier should ever be extended into and over the tide-water of the Commonwealth.

It was prescribed by the said Act —

" SEC. 3. No wharf, pier, or building, or incumbrance of any kind, shall ever hereafter be extended beyond the said line into or over the tide-water in said harbor.

" SEC. 4. No person shall enlarge or extend any wharf or pier, which is now erected on the inner side of said line further towards the said line, than such wharf or pier now stands, or than the same might have been lawfully enlarged or extended before the passing of this act, without leave first obtained in due form of law.

" SEC. 5. No person shall in any other part of the said harbor of Boston, belonging to the Commonwealth, erect or cause to be erected any wharf or pier, or begin to erect any wharf or pier therein, or place any stones, wood, or other materials in said harbor, or dig down or remove any of the land covered with water at low tide, in said harbor, with intent to erect any wharf or pier therein, or to enlarge or extend any wharf or pier now erected: *provided, however,* that nothing herein contained shall be construed as intended to restrain or control the lawful rights of the owners of any lands or flats in said harbor.

" SEC. 6. Every person offending against the provisions of this act shall be deemed guilty of a misdemeanor, and shall be liable to be prosecuted therefor, by indictment or information, in any court of competent jurisdiction, and on conviction shall be punished by a fine not less than one thousand dollars, nor more than five thousand dollars, for every offence, and any erection or obstruction which shall be made, contrary to the provisions and intent of this act, shall be liable to be removed and abated as a public nuisance, in the manner heretofore provided, for the removal and abatement of nuisances on the public highways."

The second Commission, consisting of H. A. S. Dearborn, James F. Baldwin, and Caleb Eddy, was appointed by Governor Everett, under a resolve of the Legislature passed April 9, 1839,

APPENDIX.

"To cause to be taken a copy of the survey of the harbor of Boston, made by Commissioners, under a resolve, approved the fifth day of March, one thousand eight hundred and thirty-five, and upon such copy or survey define such lines as they shall think expedient to establish, beyond which no wharves shall be extended into and over the tide-waters of the Commonwealth, on either side of said harbor : *provided*, that so much of the line as is defined by an act, approved the nineteenth day of April, one thousand eight hundred and thirty-seven, shall be considered the established line for that part of the harbor."

From their report, submitted December 28, 1839, the following extracts are made : —

"The hydrographical features of Boston Harbor, including its whole expanse, from the open ocean to the extremities of the channels, bays, and estuaries, as far as the tide flows, are so very extensive and diversified, so peculiar is the topography of its numerous islands and of the circumjacent country, — so recondite, complicated and difficult of solution are many of the laws relating to fluids, and so uncertain are the results which may be produced by any diminution of the whole area, or change in the width, depth, or direction of any of the channels, by artificial means, that questions of the gravest import are presented, for rigid investigation and profound consideration, whenever bounds are to be prescribed, beyond which, no obstructions shall be placed, that may, in any manner, impede, or divert from their natural and ancient course, the movements of the tides.

"Within this immense haven are numerous large and expensive commercial, naval, military and manufacturing establishments, as well as a vast amount of navigation of every denomination, to each and all of which particular portions, or the entire expanse of water, is immediately or indirectly important; but in a special manner as regards a free passage to and from the ocean, equal at least to that which has hitherto been enjoyed, and is indispensable for all the purposes, that induced the location of the numerous works which have either been completed, are in progress, or have been projected, and the successful prosecution of that diversified, prosperous and valuable maritime industry, for which the requisite natural facilities have been so abundantly and completely afforded.

"There are no problems in engineering, whose comprehension, solution and practical illustration have so entirely frustrated all the attempts of the most ingenious and scientific, as those which arise in the construction of hydraulic works, or in efforts to improve the navigation of rivers and harbors by the erection of piers, dams, jetties, break-waters and dikes, or the removal of impediments, for a more free and copious current of water.

APPENDIX.

"The experiments of the most enlightened nations of antiquity and of the most learned and accomplished engineers of modern times, both in Europe and in this country, for the accomplishment of those great objects which are either demanded to afford protection, and give facilities to commercial operations, or as a motive power for manufacturing or other purposes, have often failed in producing the anticipated results, from causes, which had been accidentally neglected or were disregarded, from their supposed insignificance, or which had not been sufficiently investigated and understood, or are still incapable of satisfactory explanation."

"As late as 1798, the island called 'Nick's Mate,' was so large as to be used as a sheep pasture, but it has long since been so entirely destroyed, that only a reef of rocks, visible at low water, designates its position, and on which it has been necessary to erect a monument, as a landmark for mariners.

"By a chart of the harbor, which was executed in 1775, Bird Island appears to have existed at that time; but long after the settlement of Boston, it was so extensive, as to have afforded an ample site for a spacious fort, which was for many years maintained as one of the chief military defences of the city; — now nothing remains but an extensive shoal, a very small portion of which is bare at low water.

"From a statement made to one of the Commissioners, by the late gallant captain John Forster Williams, a few years before his death, that portion of the main channel, called the 'Narrows,' which passes between Lovel's and Gallop's islands, where the Magnifique, a French seventy-four, accidentally grounded and was sunk, during the war of the revolution, had been so filled up, by the extension of the beach from the western side of the first named island, as to have been converted into solid land, and the place in which the wreck of that ship is buried, is not, at this time, overflowed at high water, by the ordinary tides.

"When an examination was made of Deer Island by the officers of the city, and other persons who were invited to accompany them, for the purpose of obtaining facts, to be included in a memorial to Congress, representing the importance of protecting, by a sea-wall, that vast natural break-water from total demolition, it was ascertained, from comparing the existing area, with that which appeared to have been its extent, by a survey which had been made about an hundred years anterior, that at least sixty acres had been washed away, by the perpetual action of the sea.

"When the French fleet, under the command of Count D'Estaing, took refuge in Nantasket Roads, after the partial action with the British squadron under Lord Howe, and encountering a severe gale off Newport, in the autumn of seventeen hundred and seventy-eight, a large field-work was erected on the eastern side of George's Island, for the protection of the ships, against an anticipated attack from those of the enemy, which appeared off the harbor; but so powerful and rapid has been the action of the waves in violent storms, upon that portion of the island, that the lofty compact, and solid earth has so far disappeared, as to leave only a few feet of the sod-work of one of the salient angles of the most western bastion.

" But nearly every island and head-land presents the effects of these causes, at distant and different periods of time, which are still in operation for their destruction, on some portions of their shores. Steep acclivities are to be seen, which are sodded over from their summits to their bases, denoting the ravages which had anciently been made, during a long succession of years, until a new direction was given, in some inexplicable manner, to the current, and the violent action of the waves, which had impinged upon and gradually worn them away; and now, not merely shoals or bars, but dry beaches, and in some cases large tracts of land covered with vegetation, extend into the harbor, from these lofty banks, while on the opposite shore, or at some other points of the same islands and promontories, a like process of devastation is going on with equally striking consequences.

With these numerous and well-established facts, it is obvious, that the changes which are continually being produced throughout the harbor result from the causes which have been named; and that any artificial means which may be employed to vary, accelerate, impede or prevent the action of any of them, may have a salutary or injurious effect, at some of the most important points in the harbor; as it is extremely difficult, if not impossible, to predict from scientific principles, or data, sufficiently numerous and conclusive, what will be the precise effect of any enlargement or diminution of the volume of water, at any particular points of the harbor. But it may be assumed, as an important and well-established element in the inquiry, that whatever is done that shall reduce the quantity of water, that passes into the large estuaries and bays, north, west and south of the city, and now covers the vast extent of shoals in other parts of the harbor, will have a direct tendency to create obstructions at some points, in the various channels, while at others the depths may be deepened, according to the manner in which the diminution of the volume of water may be occasioned, in these immense basins. This may be effected in two modes. First, by filling up portions of these capacious reservoirs, and converting so much of their areas into solid land; and second, by contracting the channels, through which the water flows into and out of them, during the flux and reflux of the tides.

" By the former mode, all the channels below would gradually be contracted in width and depth, from the sediment which would be accumulated in them, in consequence of the abated influence of the tides; and by the latter, while the immediate effect would be, to deepen those narrowed channels, from the increased velocity thus occasioned in their currents, the debris which was thereby removed would be deposited at other places, more or less remote from the ocean, according to the violence of the action which may be given to the receding waters.

" From these considerations, it has been deemed of the first consequence, that bounds should be established, beyond which obstructions should not be extended into any portions of the harbor, so far as it could be done, without a direct infringement of private rights, and a due regard to the general weal.

" But such is the imperiously increasing demand for greater accommodations, by all the branches of the infinitely varied industry, in which the accumulating population of the metropolis is employed, that it is impossible to meet it, without yielding much of mere theory, to the practical advantages which will be gained, from the increased facilities which such encroachments are intended to afford.

" It is as true, in relation to commercial emporiums as of nations, that they cannot remain stationary; they must advance or retrograde in population, affluence, consequence and grandeur; and these latter glorious results are dependent upon the active industry, intelligence, and enterprise of the former; and as the continual enlargement of maritime cities is alternately the happy cause and admirable effect of their own and their country's prosperity, whatever can be accomplished, that shall tend to produce such triumphant consequences, it is the dictate of wisdom to attempt, and if, unfortunately, any of the anticipated injurious effects, upon the capacity of Boston harbor, should be experienced, from any prospective reclamations, which may be made from its domains, it is highly probable, that the immense advantages which will have been thus derived, will warrant the experiment, and justify the expenditures, which may thereby be rendered necessary, to obviate or remove every impediment, which such encroachments may have produced, to the free navigation of the various channels, by the usual artificial means which have been resorted to, in other ages and nations; for it would not be considered an enlightened and patriotic policy, to establish the limits of a flourishing commercial capital, beyond which it should not be enlarged, from a presumed apprehension that injury, in some unknown manner, might possibly be thus done, to the natural features of its harbor. That very intelligence, enterprise, and wealth, which had been employed in laying its foundations, and rearing it to its present flourishing condition, would be directed to render all the chief approaches from the ocean, and the interior havens, roads, anchorages, and docks, commensurate with the increased wants of the expanded population and business."

In accordance with the liberal views of the Commissioners, several lines were recommended, and established by an Act of the Legislature, passed, March 17, 1840, with the same restrictions and liabilities as those attached to the Act of 1837. Said lines are fully described in the Ordinances of the city of Boston, p. 158 to 163, and appear upon the plan attached to this report.

By an Act passed March 6, 1841, the line between West Boston bridge and the Boston and Roxbury mill dam was altered in part, as described, pages 163 and 164 of the City Ordinances; a further alteration was made by Act of May 3, 1850, described in the City Ordinances, page 170, and it appears as altered upon the plan.

The third Commission was appointed under a resolve of the Legislature, passed March 22, 1845 —

" To take or cause to be taken, as soon as practicable, accurate surveys of South Bay, Charles River, and Mystic River and Pond; (above and beyond the limits prescribed to Commissioners heretofore appointed for the survey of Boston Harbor, under a resolve passed on the fifth day of March, in the year one thousand eight hundred and thirty-five,) to extend to the head of tide water on each, and embrace the marshes and flats which are overflowed by the spring tides in either; for the security of the said rivers and bay, as reservoirs essential to the continuance and capacity of Boston Harbor for commercial purposes, as well as the facilities of inland navigation and ship-building, now afforded by said rivers or either of them," with directions to " report how far, and to what extent, if any, the said bay and rivers, or either of them, may be curtailed or diminished without endangering the harbor of Boston, and greatly impairing the advantages of navigation and ship-building on said rivers: " also " to report if there be any means whereby the capacity and beneficial action of said reservoirs upon the harbor may be enlarged and increased."

The report submitted by the Commissioners, Messrs. James Hayward and Ezra Lincoln, Jr., contains much valuable information in regard to the area of the marshes and flats covered by tide-water; and the opinion of the Commissioners, contained in the following extracts, as to the importance of the great reservoirs, and the probable effect of certain improvements, upon the main channels in the harbor, deserves attention.

South Bay.

" The Commissioners find that the area of South Bay,—above the old South Boston Bridge,— is at present 345 acres. This area is about 75 or 80 acres larger than formerly, the bordering marsh land having been excavated for the purpose of filling up the South Cove and other neighboring flats. And 196 acres of marsh still remains connected with this bay. The channel above this bridge, is of small dimensions at low water, being nowhere more than 300 feet wide; and, except in the neighborhood of the bridge, not generally more than 100 feet in width. Of these 345 acres, from 250 to 300 are liable to be filled up by the owners, and will undoubtedly be so filled, to the entire exclusion of the tide. There are contracts already existing for enclosing, this very year, some 40 acres of these flats, with half as many acres of marsh, with a view to filling them up some feet above high water mark: as the demand in that neighborhood for building ground increases, other proprietors of flats will undoubtedly do the same; and, not many years hence, this bay will probably be reduced to one quarter of its present area.

" With a proper disposition of the channels and flats below, it is believed that this reduction of the area of South Bay, will have no prejudicial effect on the main channel of the harbor. If the flats east of Fore or Fort Point Channel were placed in the custody of some responsible agency,—to be filled up or otherwise disposed of, with an intelligent view to the *improvement* of commercial accommodation in the port of Boston,—there is no doubt that they can be so disposed of, as that the entire extinction of South Bay, as a part of the scouring apparatus of the main channel, would be no detriment to the harbor. The true principle is, to preserve a proper balance between the capacity of the channel and the area of the tidal rivers and bays above, to be filled and emptied twice every 24 hours through this channel. In the present state of things, Fort Point Channel would undoubtedly suffer by a very great reduction of the capacity of South Bay; but if the wall which was proposed to be built on its eastern margin were erected, it would counteract, to a great degree, the inconvenient effect of such reduction.

APPENDIX.

Mystic River.

"The area of Mystic River, above Chelsea Bridge, is 878 acres; the area of marshes adjacent, is 1,533 acres; and, if we add to these the area of Mystic Pond, which is 228 acres, we have, for the whole area within the banks, 1,106 acres; and when the tides are high enough to cover the whole of the marshes, the water surface above Chelsea Bridge is 2,639 acres. It should be remarked, however, that at *neap tides* there is no flood tide setting into Mystic Pond. The bottom of the channel at the outlet is near the level of high water at these tides, and being composed of a coarse and compact gravel, is not worn away by the action of the water, and, consequently, is not in a situation to receive the tide water at neap tides. If it should be found desirable to employ a greater scouring power in this river, the channel at the outlet might be enlarged at a comparatively small expense, to the size of the river half a mile below. Whether the owners of the outlet, and those interested in the navigation of the river, have a right to change the character of Mystic Pond, as it would be by opening such a channel, is not the province of this Commission to determine. The pond is in two divisions, which are not very different in area, and which are united by a strait which is fordable in all states of the water. The lower division of this pond is somewhat brackish. It receives the water from the river below at high water at spring tides—which water is diluted by being mingled with the waters discharged from the pond; yet, notwithstanding its freshened character, it is heavier than the waters of the pond, and occupies the lowest place. On the return of the tide, the top water is discharged from the pond; so that the southern division has become permanently brackish, notwithstanding the perpetual influx of fresh water from the river above. If the channel at the present outlet were to be enlarged, so as to give the same freedom of influx and efflux here as in the river below, this southern division of the pond would soon be very much like the river below as to the character of its waters; and the same process which is now constantly going on at the outlet, would be daily taking place at the *narrows*, or whatever the strait is called which divides the pond,—and the whole pond would, probably, in a few years, become entirely unfit for any other use than that of a basin to receive and discharge the tides of the river.

Aside from the damage that such a change in the waters of this pond would do the bordering estates, we are not quite satisfied that such an experiment is altogether desirable in itself. The velocity of the currents in the various parts of the river would be variously increased by the change, and in some parts to a very inconvenient extent. If the channel in the upper section of the river, and into the pond, could be so enlarged that the whole pond would be discharged and filled by every ebb and flood—as the river itself is now—the amount of water passing Chelsea Bridge, in ordinary tides, would be increased 25 per cent. The quantity passing Malden Bridge would be increased 47 per cent.; the increase at the rail-road bridge would be 73 per cent.; at Ten Hills Farm the quantity passing would be doubled; and at the mouth of the river proper—at the spur of Winter Hill—120 per cent. more water would pass each tide than does at present. That this additional quantity of water should pass, each tide, *through the present channel*, it would require the average velocity of the current, in these various places, to be increased in the *same ratio*. Suppose that the average velocity of the current at half tide, at the Boston and Maine Rail-road Bridge, to be now 4 feet per second; by making the change proposed, the current at the same place, (on the supposition that the pond is emptied and filled each tide through the present channel,) must be 7 feet per second. Or, suppose that at half flood now, in a given tide, the average velocity at the narrows, the spur of Winter Hill, is 5 feet per second—it would, in the case supposed, become 11 feet per second. And in any section of the river higher up, the change would be proportionally greater. The bottom and sides of the present channel are not adapted to this changed state of the current. Portions of the bed and banks of the river, which have hitherto resisted the action of the water, would yield to this increased action, and incalculable changes in the channel itself would be the consequence.

"We are of opinion, however, that, if this experiment were tried, the results above stated would not be realized to their full extent—as, in the present state of the channel, the pond would not be filled and discharged to the present compass of the tides in the river—and, consequently, the actual velocity of the current would not be as great as is stated in the above hypothesis. But the velocity of the current must be very much increased by such an addition to the capacity of the reservoir; and, probably, large portions of the present bed and banks of the river would be removed from the narrower parts, and carried down and deposited in the wider parts below the Ten Hills Farm. The river in this part being eight or ten times as wide as it is at the narrows, and above, the velocity of the current on the ebb, is, of course, deadened by the expanded character of the channel; and the marsh mud and other material which the current, in its increased velocity, may be able to carry with it, will be deposited, and the formation of a shoal or bar be the undoubted result. This process would go on till the river had acquired a *permanent state;* that is, till the capacity of the channel should be so enlarged, and (for the same reason) the velocity of the current should be so diminished, that the sides and bed of the river would be able to resist the further action of the water.

Charles River.

"The area of Charles River above Charles River Bridge, within its banks, including Miller's River, (the estuary bank of East Cambridge,) and the bay back of the State Prison, is, in all, 1,340 acres. The amount of marsh land connected with it, and overflowed at spring tides, is 915 acres.

That part of Charles River between Warren Bridge and the Brookline branch of the Mill Dam road, and which, for the sake of distinction, we call *Cambridge Bay*, has a deep and spacious channel as far up as the cross dam of the Boston Water Power Company. From thence to the mouth of the river proper, which is about half a mile, there are shoals which have been caused, undoubtedly, by the diminished current, occasioned by the sudden expansion of the river at that place, into the broad bay above mentioned. From the Charles River Bridge to a point about 1,000 feet southwesterly of West Boston Bridge, there is from 15 to 20 feet of water in the channel at low water—and, in many places, a greater depth; but from the last mentioned point to the *Cross Dam* beforementioned, the channel shoals away; and thence to the mouth of the river proper, it is broken, and has not more than three or four feet of water at low water.

"From this point upwards, Charles River has a much better channel than Mystic River. It has, in the neighborhood of its mouth, from 10 to 15 feet of water at low water. And it maintains a much greater regularity in its character, quite up to the head of tide water, than does the corresponding part of Mystic River. The average height of high water at the bridge near the Old Village in Cambridge,—which has been always called "*Cambridge Bridge*," and which was long the only bridge over the channel of Charles River below Watertown, (there are now eleven,) is two inches; and that at the bridge near the arsenal in Watertown, is four inches higher than high water at the Navy Yard. And the average compass of the tides in this river, is very nearly the same that it is at Charlestown. The bay or shoal at the head of Cambridge Bay, the mouth of the river proper, is the principal impediment to navigation. The most feasible way of removing this is by the dredging machine.

"The importance of this river and bay, and that of the Mystic, to the preservation of the main channel, down to the islands, are altogether incalculable. They are the two main arteries which literally supply the life current of Boston Harbor. And the Commissioners would respectfully recommend to the Legislature the preservation of these estuaries, to the greatest extent that may be consistent with the rights of individual proprietors of bordering estates.

"If the modern construction of the colonial law of 1641, that 'the riparian proprietor has a right to exclude the tide water from the flats in front of his estate, to the distance of one hundred rods, if there be no intervening channel;' if this modern construction of the law must prevail, then Boston Harbor is in danger of serious injury. This subject is one which commends itself to the careful consideration of the Legislature. The whole State has an interest in it. The preservation of Boston, as a place of trade, of commerce, of ships,—is every year increasing in importance to the whole northern section of the country. Every part of New England has its rail-roads running to this city. These have been built for purposes of business, of trade. They connect the interior of the country with the commerce of the world. But, annihilate the harbor of Boston, and these expensive facilities for inter-communication will become of little value either to the city or the country."

" We have spoken of the importance of these two large estuaries, as means of preservation to the great channel which constitutes what may be called the main trunk of the inner harbor. We beg leave to suggest a few considerations touching the main channel itself.

" This channel commences at the junction of Charles and Mystic Rivers, opposite the Navy Yard, and extends southeasterly about three and a half miles, opening into the lower harbor between Fort Independence and Fort Warren. From its mouth between these two islands, to the Cunard Wharf, this channel is very straight, and of a clear width of about 3000 feet. Before the extension of the wharves at East Boston, the width of this channel in the narrowest point was about 1700 feet. It has been considerably curtailed by the extension of wharves and other fixtures, particularly at East Boston. The Commissioners would respectfully suggest that the channel between East Boston and the city proper is, in their opinion, to be treated with great care and caution; that it should not be unnecessarily narrowed. In the extension of wharf accommodations at East Boston, it would be well to build on the west side of the island, opposite the Navy Yard, and along the southeastern side towards Bird Island. But the further encroachment upon the main channel opposite the city proper, and opposite to the flats at the mouth of Fort Point Channel, should be avoided,—at least, till a more urgent necessity arises than exists at present; and till there shall be opportunity to observe the effects of encroachments upon that channel already made.

" The building of new wharves, the extension of old ones—the filling up of flats to the exclusion of the tide, and the consequent diversion of the currents to a greater or less degree, are producing changes in the state of the harbor, some of them innocent, some of them more or less detrimental to its character, and some of them tending to serious consequences. Changes of this kind have been observed since the survey made in 1835. Some of these are traceable to particular causes, and tend to throw light on the general subject of causes and effects in relation to these changes. They all show the importance of having the harbor *taken care of*—of having it in the *custody* of some responsible authority, which shall insure the requisite watchfulness and care —a commission emanating from the Legislature; that it should be the duty of such a commission to see that the works permitted to be erected on the borders of the harbor, or within its channels, should be so constructed as to do no injury, or the least possible injury, to the same; that they should be what they were authorized to be, and nothing more. That the said commission should keep a careful record of all such changes in the structures and fixtures in and about the harbor. That plans should be taken of all such structures, upon such a scale as will readily show what the structure is, particularly in relation to its tendencies and effect upon the tides, the channels, and the facilities of navigation. That the result of these alterations should be carefully observed, and recorded for after reference and comparison; and, that such observations and experiments upon the motions, magnitude and effects of the tides, as will show the tendencies of the existing state of things, be made on such occasions, and at such intervals, as will furnish the desired information."

The lines recommended by the Commissioners in Charles River, Miller's River, and South Bay, were, by an Act passed April 26, 1847, established as the lines in Boston Harbor beyond which no wharf or pier should ever be extended into and over the tide-water of the Commonwealth. Said lines are fully described in the Ordinances of the City, pages 164, 165, and appear upon the plan.*

Fourth Commission—under a resolve of the Legislature, approved April 16, 1846—Messrs. Joseph Bell and Ezra Lincoln, Jr., were appointed Commissioners

" To ascertain what private rights will be affected by adopting the precautions and restrictions recommended and pointed out in

* 1847, Ch. 34, (April 7,) appropriation of $3,500 to procure a chart of Boston Harbor, by the Officers and Engineers of the United States engaged in the Coast Survey.

the report and plans of the commissioners appointed for the survey of the South Bay, Charles River, Mystic River and Pond,—what is the value of those rights, and what amount of compensation will be required by the proprietors for the necessary interference with them ;" " also, to examine the wharves and other structures that have been built or extended on the borders of the harbor of Boston, or within its channels, by permission from the Legislature, granted since the establishment of the line recommended by the commissioners in the year 1837, or otherwise, and to report the facts in all cases of violation of the law."

In respect to private claims, after an able examination of the law, the Commissioners arrive at the following conclusion : —

" It seems entirely clear, therefore, that the colonial ordinance of 1641, has now the force, under our constitution, of a statute within that portion of the Commonwealth formerly constituting the Colony of Massachusetts Bay. By this, therefore, as a rule of property, all the flats within the scope of the present inquiry are fully embraced, and must be finally determined.

" The judicial decisions, also, on this subject, within the Commonwealth, from an early period have been founded on, and, so far as they have gone, been in accordance with this ordinance.

" The rights of the sovereign, by the common law, have given place, to a certain extent, to the rights of the riparian owner, and a qualified ownership has been constituted between high and low water mark, in him, to the extent of 100 rods, on the sole condition that such owner shall not, in the language of the proviso, ' by this liberty have power to stop or hinder the passage of boats or other vessels in or through any sea, creeks or coves, to other men's houses or lands.'

" The precise legal bearing or extent of this proviso, has not, so far as the undersigned have been able to learn, been the subject of any final and exact judicial determination.

" But, construing the grant and the proviso together, as they must be, both being equally in force, and constituting together an important rule of property, it seems clear, that while important public rights have been surrendered to the private owners of adjoining upland, still other and important rights are reserved to the public. The exact divisional line or the precise extent of the rights granted and the rights retained, depending, as they do, upon the construction of an act of legislation, rests with the judicial department of the government, when properly presented ; and until such determination shall be had, it will not be reasonable to expect any great degree of certainty or accuracy in estimating the comparative value each may respectively claim in this species of property."

In pursuing their investigations, with a view to discover all cases of violation of the law, they examined carefully the several Acts establishing lines in the harbor, as well as the numerous Acts granting leave to individuals and corporations to extend separate wharves to said lines, and caused the lines about the City proper, East Boston, South Boston, and Charlestown, to be accurately re-surveyed. The Commissioners reported no less than twenty-three cases of infringements of the law. In reference to this subject, the following resolve was passed by the Legislature :—

Resolved, That the District Attorney for the County of Suffolk be, and he is hereby directed, by filing information, by indictment or other process, to abate nuisances, and to enforce penalties that have been, or shall be, incurred, by any violation of the law passed on the nineteenth day of April, 1837, entitled " an Act to preserve the Harbor of Boston, and to prevent encroachments therein," and of any subsequent law made for the same purpose. Approved April 26, 1847.

February 17, 1848, an order was passed directing the committee on mercantile affairs, &c., to inquire " whether any, and, if any, what measures have been taken to carry into effect the resolve of April 26, 1847.

In their report the Committee insert a letter from Samuel D. Parker, Attorney of the Commonwealth for Suffolk County, from which the following extract is made :—

" If the prosecutions contemplated were to be in the form of informations, I can also state that my attention has not been called to the subject by any body ; and, to this very hour, I am informed of no intrusion, except the Boston Wharf Company's, against whom a temporary injunction was, before 1847, ordered by the supreme court, and an old indictment is still pending, in the municipal court. I have never seen, nor been served with, a copy of the report of the legislative committee, mentioning the intrusions, if there be such a report, or of the names of the intruders, which you spoke of ; and I do not understand the resolve to cast on me the duty of surveyor, or to go on a hunting excursion all along the commissioner's line, which itself is not, as far as I know, made visible by inspection.

" Under these circumstances, neither the grand juries, by indictments, nor I, by informations, have done anything in the premises."

By a resolve of the Legislature, approved May 10, 1848, the Secretary of the Commonwealth was directed to furnish, without delay, an attested copy of the report made by Joseph Bell and Ezra Lincoln, Jr., to the Attorney of the Commonwealth for the county of Suffolk, and to the Attorney for the Northern District; and the said Attorneys were required, without delay, to prosecute all violations of the law passed April 19, 1837, and any subsequent law made for the same purpose.

Upon receipt of the certified documents referred to, the County Attorney addressed letters to the Mayor and Aldermen, the City Solicitor, the City Marshal, the Harbor Master, the Boston Marine Society, and to such private individuals as, in his judgment, might be able to furnish information upon the subject.

A circular was then prepared by the County Attorney, and addressed to all the parties infringing upon the law—in consequence of which, nearly all the cases were satisfactorily adjusted, the wharves being reduced to their proper limits—four only remain unsettled; three of these are still before the supreme court.

Fifth Commission—
Under authority of a resolve of the Legislature, passed April 16, 1846. Governor Briggs appointed Messrs. Thomas G. Carey, Simeon Borden, and Ezra Lincoln, Jr., Commissioners

" To examine the position of the flats in the Harbor of Boston, between South Boston and the Channel, and lying opposite to the wharves on Sea and Broad Streets, with a view to ascertain whether any improvement can be made thereof beneficial to the commerce of Boston, and to report such a plan of improvement as may appear to them to be feasible and judicious ; and whether it would be beneficial to straiten the Commissioners' line between Arch Wharf and Wales's Wharf."

The Commissioners' Report is dated 2d of February, 1847. With the assistance of Dr. Bache, Superintendent of the United States Coast Survey, they obtained a valuable chart of the flats in question, based upon scientific triangulation and accurate soundings; and after repeated examinations of the flats and channels, and also of the lower harbor, for the purpose of ascertaining what would be the probable effect, either above or below, of any changes that have been proposed, they say—

"The flats in question, lying between a line 1650 feet from high water mark, above referred to, and a line or lines hereinafter described, beyond which the commissioners do not deem it expedient to enclose, cover a surface of about 360 acres, extending from Fort Point Channel, on the south side of the city, to the continuation of the easterly line of the enclosure used for the South Boston institutions, and in front of the whole shore of South Boston. They are covered, at each ordinary tide, to the depth of about ten feet. If the whole area of the flats opposite the shore of South Boston were situated above the city, receiving the tide through any channel by which vessels must pass to reach their places of discharge, there can be no question that it would be extremely dangerous to the commerce of the port to enclose them. To exclude from such a basin a volume of water that aids to scour the channel in the upper harbor, as it passes to and from the sea four times a day, might produce changes of the most injurious character. The enclosure of the back bay, as it is called, by the Western Avenue, is an instance of this kind which it would be hazardous to repeat. But the flats in question lie *below* the city. The water that covers them aids in no such scouring process. That process is, in fact, somewhat diminished in its effect, by suffering a portion of the water that daily ascends, as a supply for the upper basins, to flow over so wide a surface instead of confining its passage to the channels.

" This opinion is corroborated by the observations of Lieut. Charles H. Davis, the officer at the head of the hydrographical party, by whom the data for the chart accompanying this report were furnished. He says, in a letter to the commissioners, giving the result of his daily observations upon the tides and currents in the inner harbor, that 'the ebb tide crosses the northeast end of the South Boston flats; and, on looking at the chart, you will perceive that this is its necessary course,—the northeast end of the flats running further out into the ship channel than any other part.' 'Near slack water, both of ebb and flood, the tide flows broad over the flats, but with a velocity so small, that it is inappreciable, and with no general or determinate direction.'"

"The commissioners are, therefore, of opinion, that no evil would ensue from giving permission to build any solid structures on these flats, that may be required for commercial purposes. On the other hand, if a sea-wall or line of wharves were erected, at a suitable distance from that edge of these flats which makes one side of Fort Point Channel, and if a similar barrier were made on the side towards the main channel, in the opinion of the commissioners, the current in each channel would be rather quickened, and its depth more securely preserved by the change.

"In order to prevent any injury to the wharves already erected on the Boston side of Fort Point Channel, by cutting off such passage as it is found convenient to use over the flats in their present state, as well as for the general improvement of that channel and the main ship channel, the commissioners are of opinion, that, whenever the flats in question are enclosed or built upon, as above suggested, the whole area on the exterior of the lines above described should be excavated, to a depth of ten feet below the plane of reference for the soundings on the chart presented. In their view, also, no extension beyond the line of 1650 feet from the high-water mark should be permitted, unless the party or parties so extending should be under obligation to excavate to the depth above specified, from the end of his or their structure to deep water, and to cut off the northerly point of the flats outside of the line drawn for enclosure from Fort Point channel to the main ship channel. In order to be certain of the practicability of such an excavation, the commissioners have had the whole area of flats, beyond the line of 100 rods from high water mark, carefully sounded by men of experience in such work, and they have found nothing but strata of clay and loose sand, which can be easily removed by the excavating machines now in common use. This excavation should be made at the expense of those who may be suffered to build upon the flats, if such permission should be given to any party. And it is believed that the facilities and convenience which such an excavation would afford to vessels passing into or out of Fort Point channel, at all times of tide, would fully compensate the owners of wharves adjoining that channel for the loss of the privilege of passing over the flats with vessels of light draught at high water. It would seem that these owners, if they were not thus secured against injury by the change proposed, would be entitled to an indemnity; on the same principle on which they would be entitled to compensation if a bridge should be thrown across Fort Point channel, to connect any enclosure on the flats with the city.

" In regard to the lower harbor, the quantity of water that enters to cover this shoal of flats, extensive as it is, is scarcely appreciable, when considered in relation to the great flood that approaches from the sea to fill the harbor at every tide. And, in the opinion of the commissioners, the enclosure can produce no perceptible effect on the outer channels in any way. If it were otherwise, they would discourage any plan of alteration, believing, as they do, that no change should be permitted, that could diminish the depth of channel below. They have given careful attention to that subject, and, after personal examination of the points of danger, they present some considerations that seem to them important in framing any measures that may be proposed for the security of the harbor. In making laws that are intended for this purpose, a careful discrimination of the causes from which injury proceeds, and intelligence in applying the remedy, are peculiarly necessary. Otherwise, as has been the case heretofore, onerous restrictions may be imposed, that have no tendency to stop the mischief; and the community are left under false security, in the belief that nothing more is necessary, when, in truth, nothing has been effected.

" Some of the islands and headlands in the harbor are gradually wasting away by the action of the sea, and some of the shoals are found to be increasing. One change is probably the cause of the other. The earth and small stones, that are loosened from the headlands, are carried by the currents and lodged upon the adjacent shoals, which are generally extended by these additions. Whenever this waste of the headlands is stopped, by suitable protection from the sea, the increase of the shoals must cease, since the materials by which they are extended will no longer be supplied. In the meantime, the removal of small stones for ballast from the headlands must be injurious, as it hastens their waste. But the removal of such stones from the shoals to which they have been carried by the action of the current, after being detached from the headland, can do no injury. It may rather be beneficial, by retarding the increase of shoals, if it diminishes what aids to form them.

" A more particular description of these changes, and their causes, is as follows: The elements which combine to destroy or waste the islands and headlands above referred to, are the waters of the ocean, agitated by strong winds and storms, and the various tidal currents. These elements act upon the headlands somewhat in the following manner. Almost every island and headland is more exposed to the action of the waves, when the wind blows from some particular quarter or point of the compass, than when it blows in any other direction. If the wind to which the coast is most exposed be a prevailing wind, and, at the same time, has a tendency to increase the height of tides when it blows strongly for any considerable length of time, its destructive operations will be greater than if its tendency were to prevent high tides; as the action of the waves, during the full spring tides, has a more destructive influence than during the neap tides. For the purpose of illustrating our views, we will suppose the shores of an island, or headland, to be of two or three miles in extent, extending in a north and south direction, and more exposed to the action of the waves when the wind blows from the northeast, than from any other quarter. We will now suppose the northeast wind to be a prevailing wind upon the coast, and frequently blowing very heavy. It will be obvious to every person, who has witnessed the dashing of heavy waves upon a beach or shore, that the tendency of each successive wave is to move the sand and small shingle, upon the surface of the beach in the direction in which the wave itself rolls; and the tendency of the under-tow, as it is called, is to roll or wash the shingle and sand, in a line at a right angle with the direction of the beach, towards the ocean, or low-water mark. A succeeding wave again rolls it obliquely towards high-water mark; when the under-tow again takes it back in a perpendicular direction. The action of successive waves, continued for any considerable length of time, particularly if aided by a tidal current, will remove the shingle and sand, composing the surface of the beach, from the northerly end of the island, or headland, towards the south, until the shingle is nearly, if not all, swept off, leaving the finer and lighter particles of the primitive earth exposed to the action of the waves. This action will mix them with the waters of the ocean; and they will be taken away by the tidal currents, and be gradually deposited, in proportion to their specific gravities, the minuteness of their division, and the motion or agitation of the water in which they are suspended. Long continued operations of this kind will undermine the headland banks, and cause them to tumble into the sea; the grosser particles covering the beach with sand and shingle, while the finer parts are mixed with the waters, and taken away in the manner above-mentioned. In this manner, will the sand and shingle-gravel continue to be swept along the beach, until they reach the end of it. They will not remain at rest, until they arrive at a point beyond the influence of the waves. There they will form shoals, and frequently beaches of great length. Sometimes these operations are somewhat counteracted by the equal exposure of the headlands to winds having opposite effects. The sand, in this case, will be sometimes moved in one direction, and sometimes in another. The tendency will be, to afford a more constant covering of the beach with sand and gravel, which constitute its natural protection against the wasting influence of the waves. In cases of this sort, the effect is, usually, the formation of two shoals and beaches one at each end of the headland. In the winter season, when the northerly winds prevail, the shoals at the south will increase; and in summer, when the southerly winds prevail, the shoals at the north will increase.

"The commissioners, entertaining the views above expressed, believe that the unfavorable changes which are going on in the harbor, are not of a nature to be affected by any new structure that may be erected on the flats lying in front of South Boston; the outward changes having been probably produced solely by causes that have arisen in the lower harbor itself. They believe those causes, however, to demand serious and early attention, beginning, as they appear to do, with the waste of headlands on which the security of our navigation depends, and requiring only suitable defences and short breakwaters to preserve the channels.

"In respect to a plan for the occupation of the flats in question, the commissioners suppose that it would be premature, and of little use, to present any design or drawing in detail, until it shall be decided whether the right to occupy that portion of the area which remains under the control of the Commonwealth, is to be united with the property on the margin of South Boston. To leave an open passage between that margin and an insulated enclosure upon the flats, might be injurious to Fort Point channel, by diminishing the volume of water that scours it towards its mouth. But, with this exception, they believe that any plan which may be found most convenient for commercial purposes, whenever more accommodation is required, may probably be adopted without injury to navigation, whether it be by an entire enclosure in sea-walls, approaching within a moderate distance of the channel, or by the extension of wharves from the South Boston shore towards the main channel, after that shore shall itself have been advanced forward upon the flats, by filling up.

"In the present state of the title to the property, therefore, they present no plan in detail. Nor can the commissioners assume the responsibility of expressing an opinion at all favorable to a change of such magnitude in the harbor, without referring to some considerations that were presented in the legislative report which recommended their appointment.

"Although the title to these flats is clearly in the Commonwealth, it is held in trust for the benefit and security of commerce;

being a right to the ground only, while the right of passage over it is common to every individual in the community. No instance is known in which the sovereign power of a state has put property of this nature into the market for sale. It may prove to be a question of serious consequence, whether the change proposed is to be made under the direction of a controlling power that regards the security of navigation as the object paramount in importance, or whether the rights of the Commonwealth are to be transferred to parties who look for a pecuniary gain, from speculation in this property, as the chief object of consideration. If these rights are to be transferred at all, the city of Boston, whose interests are inseparable from those of navigation, would seem to be the safest and most suitable depository of a trust that concerns the prosperity of the State and the commerce of the Union."

The Sixth Commission, consisting of Messrs. S. S. Lewis and Ezra Lincoln, Jr., having been appointed by Governor Briggs, under the resolve of the Legislature, passed April 7, 1847, "relating to the survey of Boston Harbor," were authorized and directed by an additional resolve, passed May 10, 1848,

"To define, upon a plan, or plans, such lines, in that portion of the harbor of Boston, lying between East Boston and Chelsea, and known as Chelsea Creek, as they shall think expedient to establish, beyond which no wharves or other structure shall be extended into and over the tide-waters of the Commonwealth; also to ascertain whether any obstructions are forming in Fort Point Channel, in the harbor of Boston, and whether any legislation is necessary to prevent or remove the same.

"The commissioners, in regard to the first requirement of the above recited resolve, to define lines, &c., in Chelsea Creek, after an examination of the same, with reference to the rights of the Commonwealth, are of opinion that this estuary of the harbor of Boston, obstructed, as it has been, by one or two solid dams above the bridge which connects East Boston with Chelsea, exercises but little scouring influence upon the main channels of the harbor. In deciding, therefore, upon lines to which wharves might be extended, without detriment to public or private rights, the commissioners were governed mainly by a desire to keep the present channel in such condition, with reference to width, &c., as to accommodate the shipping which might hereafter have to pass into and out of said creek, and, at the same time, reconcile any conflicting views which parties, owning on opposite sides of the creek, might hold.

" With this view, and in order to make the entrance of the channel easy of access, it became necessary to keep the line on the East Boston side, opposite the ferry slip of the Winnisimmet Company, above or within low-water mark some distance, as represented on the plan herewith presented, thereby cutting off a considerable area of the flats belonging to the East Boston Land Company. This arrangement, however, was assented to by the said company, and a vote of its directors was passed, sanctioning the line, and, in effect, making a dedication of the area, so cut off, to public uses.

" The lines hereinafter described, are believed to be generally satisfactory to all the riparian proprietors, and entirely consistent with all the public interests.

" In regard to the second instruction recited in the resolve passed May 10th, 1848, viz., ' to ascertain whether any obstructions are forming in Fort Point Channel, &c.,' the commissioners would observe that there is a well known bar in the vicinity of the Summer Street wharf, so called, and extending nearly across the channel aforesaid, so as to leave but a narrow passage at low-water near the South Boston flats for vessels drawing over six feet of water. This bar is indicated on the plan of the inner harbor of Boston heretofore prepared for the Commonwealth ; and the commissioners have recently sounded upon various parts of it, and found it to be about one hundred feet in width, composed of soft clay four or five feet in depth, covered with a stratum of coarse gravel. From the nature of the bottom of the channel, above and below this bar, it is believed that a deposit of the silt from the drains, which empty into the docks in this vicinity, may be made about the bar. The vessels which go up the channel are liable, at low water, to catch upon this bar, and are then obliged to wait for the turn of the tide. As the bar is, as before suggested, of a nature to be easily excavated, the commissioners are of opinion that it would greatly facilitate navigation in this channel, if it should be removed. After it has been once removed, the water, which comes down from South Bay, at every ebb tide, will unquestionably keep the channel clear ; and, as it has been proposed and recommended heretofore, by State commissioners, that the line between Wales's and Arch Wharves, should be straightened on certain conditions, the commissioners would recommend that the proprietors of wharves, in the vicinity of this line should, in case it be straightened, and, when they are permitted to extend to it, be required to remove this bar, or obstruction, in the channel."

The lines recommended by the Commissioners were established by an act of the Legislature, passed May 2, 1849—they are fully described in the Ordinances of the City, pages 166 to 170, and may be found upon the plan attached to this report.*

The seventh Board of Commissioners, appointed by the Governor and Council under a resolve of the Legislature passed May 10, 1848, —

"to consider and report to the next Legislature what are the rights and duties of the Commonwealth in relation to the flats in the harbor of Boston ; — also to consider whether the public good requires that any portion of said flats should be filled, and to what extent ; and whether the maritime interests do now, or probably may hereafter, require the excavation of any part of them to enlarge the harbor accommodations ; — and also, if it shall be deemed expedient to fill any of said flats, to report the outlines of a plan for that purpose, and the terms upon which such filling up should be authorized,"

Consisted of Messrs. John M. Williams, David Cummings, Thomas Hopkinson, George S. Boutwell, and Charles Hudson.

The comprehensive nature of the questions submitted to the commissioners warranted the general view of the subject which is taken in their report submitted in January, 1850.

They discuss at length the legal merits of the case, and say, —

"The better opinion seems to be, in England, that the king holds the land between high and low water mark, as well as under all navigable waters, in trust for the use of the people ; and though he may grant his private right to others, it must still be subject, in the hands of his grantee, to the right of all his subjects to pass and repass, without obstruction, on both the land and water. It has been supposed by some that, in analogy to this principle, the Commonwealth holds the flats over which its title

---

* Stat. 1850, Ch. 216, April 17th. The line on Fore Point Channel, between Wales's wharf and Arch wharf altered.

Stat. 1850, Ch. 254, April 30th. An Act authorizing the proprietors of several wharves, between Arch wharf and Wales's wharf to extend to the new line of Fore Point Channel, provided a certain bar in said channel, opposite the foot of Summer street, be excavated to the depth of twelve feet below low water, &c.

extends, in trust for all the people, and can only alienate them subject to this trust. But the analogy fails in two important particulars. 1st. The Commonwealth, in its sovereign capacity, possesses not only the rights and powers, on this subject, which are possessed by the king in England, but also of the British Parliament, consisting of king, lords, and commons; and it has never been doubted that Parliament, in its arrogated omnipotence, may grant an exclusive right to flats, unincumbered by the supposed trust. 2d. The Commonwealth is the public — the people — in whom, in their collective capacity, full sovereignty resides. The Commonwealth is, therefore, both the trustee and the beneficiary. The trust estate and beneficial interest are united, and consequently the trust is merged in the fee.

" Subject to the restrictions and limitations before mentioned, the Commonwealth has the full power, title and control of the flats in Boston harbor. The right to manage and dispose of them is, by the Constitution of the Commonwealth, vested in the Legislature. The Commonwealth may, by the acts and at the discretion of the Legislature, cause or permit them to be excavated or embanked, or retained, or otherwise disposed of. It may grant them to the city, to the riparian proprietors, or to other persons or corporations, at such times, in such manner, on such terms and conditions, and for such considerations of public benefit, pecuniary or otherwise, as the Legislature, in the exercise of its sound, constitutional discretion, may judge to be most proper, and most conducive to the public interest and welfare."

In considering the "duties of the Commonwealth," they pass in review the reports of the several preceding commissioners; and although they agree with their predecessors in general positions, and adopt the most of their conclusions, they differ from them entirely in regard to the policy to be pursued, as will appear from the following extracts, viz.:—

" If the South Bay were kept open to its full extent, a sea wall upon the easterly side of Fore Point Channel might quicken the current in that channel, and so increase its depth. But as the greater part of that spacious bay is, or will be, closed so as to exclude the water which has heretofore entered it, we are unable to perceive why the same causes which are allowed to operate in other parts of the harbor, may not operate here to the injury of this channel. Nor are we able to see how a sea wall on the easterly side of this channel can avert the calamity, in case South Bay should be filled up. In that case, there would be a little more than a narrow channel left open above the South Boston bridges, and no water would pass up Fore Point Channel, except what would be required to fill the narrow channel above the bridges.

"Nor is it by any means certain that filling up all the South Boston flats, — a tract of some seven or eight hundred acres, now covered by water, at every tide, to the depth of eight or ten feet, will not prove injurious to the main channels in the harbor. It was in evidence before the commissioners that there had been a great reduction in the depth of Fore Point Channel, and also in the main ship channel both in the upper and lower harbor. At the 'Narrows,' so called, in the lower harbor, it was shown that the water had shoaled from three to five feet within the last twenty or thirty years; and that though this was ascribed in a good degree to the washing away of the islands and headlands in the outer harbor, the same accretion is observable in the upper harbor, where these causes do not exist. In Fore Point Channel, at the 'Upper Middle,' and indeed in almost every part of the harbor, the channels are becoming more obstructed by becoming more shoal or more narrow. It is a well known fact, that at the wharves and in the docks there is a constant accretion of matter, so as to render it necessary to dredge them out once in four or five years.

"But the arguments against filling up these flats are met by the declaration, — that the quantity of water which would be displaced by the proposed improvements, would be so small as to be hardly appreciable upon the main currents in the harbor. But a glance at what has been done, and what may be done, by the shore owners, will show that the quantity of water which has been and may be displaced is far from being inconsiderable. Boston proper, which originally contained less than 1000 acres, now contains more than 3000 acres. This increase of more than 2000 acres has all been made by encroachments upon tide water. In addition to this, the Mill Dam cut off 700 or 800 acres more; — to this may be added the large quantity of land made at Cambridge, Charlestown, Chelsea, and East Boston. Here we have an area of several thousand acres which are forever lost to the harbor. This exclusion of tide water from so large a surface, has produced a sensible effect upon the channels in the harbor. The harbor master testified that the filling up above Charles River Bridge, has produced a visible effect upon the current between Boston and East Boston. By reducing the volume of water from Charles River, the former balance of power between the currents from the Charles and Mystic Rivers at their confluence, had been destroyed; and the consequence was, that the main current between Boston and East Boston was brought nearer to the Boston shore than it was formerly.

"But we are not to confine our attention to the three or four thousand acres of flats which have been already irrevocably lost to the harbor. By the report of Messrs. Hayward and Lincoln, in 1846, it appears that at that time the tide flowed over an area of 5000 acres above the Charles River, Chelsea and South Boston bridges; and of this 5000 acres, 2700 were above low water mark, and so were liable to be filled up by the shore owners, leaving only about 2300 acres to be flowed by the tides. It should also be borne in mind that every acre of the flats situated just above low water, is as important to the harbor, and receives and discharges as much water, as an acre in the deepest channel; it being only the water between high and low water mark which carries on the scouring process, by which the channels are kept open. When we are called upon to decide whether it would be safe to fill up eight or nine hundred acres in front of South Boston, we are to remember that one-half of this area may be filled at the pleasure of the shore owners; and the real question to be decided is, whether the State should, at the present time, authorize the filling up of some four hundred acres more, in addition to the five or six hundred acres at South and East Boston, and the twenty-seven hundred acres above the bridges, all of which may be filled by their respective owners, and much of which will probably be filled, as the demand for land is constantly increasing.

"When the subject is stripped of all its disguises, and is presented in its naked form, we are inclined to hesitate before we pronounce in favor of filling up the flats over which the State has control. When the safety of the harbor is placed in competition with any magnificent scheme of land speculation, we must decide in favor of what we believe to be the safety of the harbor. When we consider, that a volume of water, of an average depth of at least seven feet, covering an area larger than the whole city of Boston proper, is now liable to be excluded from the harbor, we want something more than a mere speculative theory of tides and channels, to justify us in adding to this quantity. When we consider, that flats once filled can never be restored to harbor accommodations; but that flats kept open, can, at any future period be filled, when it shall have been demonstrated by experience, that previous fillings have wrought no injury to the harbor, — we believe it to be the dictate of wisdom to pause before we make any further grants, except they be accompanied with an obligation to make corresponding excavations, or other improvements, in the harbor."

They submit a variety of statistics and think, —

"These facts will fully sustain the position that our commerce has tripled in the space of twenty years. And if the commerce of Boston is to go on increasing in this ratio, the day is not far distant when the flats will be wanted for dockage and anchorage of the vessels, which our growing trade will call into this port. And even now these flats are used by vessels of a light draft of water. The eastern coasters, with wood and lumber, frequently pass across the flats at high water. And it was in evidence before the commissioners, that during periods of easterly winds, when it is difficult to go to sea, there are frequently several hundreds of these small vessels, mostly from Maine and the British Provinces, lying in the harbor; and, owing to the crowded state of the channel, large numbers of them resort to the soft mud on the flats, for anchorage; — a fact that shows most conclusively, that fifty, or even twenty years hence, the very space which it is now proposed to fill up, will become absolutely necessary to accommodate the vessels in the harbor. The extreme line which has been recommended, which for the sake of distinction, we will call Mr. Carey's line, not only allows all the South Boston flats to be filled, with the exception of a small point opposite Rowe's wharf, but actually cuts off nearly two hundred acres below low water mark; — the greater portion of which, as shown by the soundings, has a depth, at extreme low water, of from three to four feet, — while some portions of the harbor, thus proposed to be cut off, have a depth of from four to seven feet; and to these soundings we may add two feet, to show the depth at mean low water. Here there are nearly two hundred acres, well adapted to the anchorage of these small coasters, which it has been proposed to fill up; but which, we are satisfied, will, in a few years, become almost indispensably necessary for this class of vessels. We, therefore, should regard it as a departure from the dictates of true wisdom, to suffer any embankment or structure to be erected upon any of the harbor belonging to the State, which can be used as a roadstead, or converted into wet docks.

"We have already stated what we believe to be the *rights* of the Commonwealth, in the flats situated between the one hundred-rod line and the channel. We have no doubt but that she has an interest, a vendible property, in these flats, which she may dispose of as she pleases, under the limitations we have stated. And what is true of the flats in Boston harbor, is true of the flats similarly situated, in every other harbor in the State. The question is not local in its character, but is coextensive with our coast. It is a subject in which the whole State has an equal interest, and hence the impolicy and injustice of granting these flats to individuals or corporations, without consideration. Neither the riparian owners, nor the city or town within whose territorial limits they may happen to be situated, can claim them in virtue of their proximity. They belong to the State, and are the property of the whole people.

"But though the State possesses this property, and the Legislature may dispose of it as they please, they are bound by every consideration of sound policy to make such a disposition of these flats as will best promote the prosperity and general welfare of the community.

" Nor will they, as guardians of the public weal, confine their views to the present condition of things. Any policy which does not look forward at least a century, and consider the wants of the people at the end of that period, is repugnant to the spirit of the age, and so dishonorable to the character of this Commonwealth. While the present wants of the people should be provided for, their future prosperity and welfare should not be overlooked. A system should be adopted, in the disposition of this property, which will meet the wants of the present generation, and at the same time subserve the interest of those who come after us. If the State, actuated by a narrow and parsimonious policy, should dispose of this property to individuals, and put the avails into her own treasury, in a short time this money would be expended, and so be forever lost to the State; while the property, passing into private hands, would be appropriated, to the perpetual injury of the harbor, and consequent detriment of the commerce of the Commonwealth. But, on the other hand, if the Legislature should hold this property in their own hands, to be appropriated from time to time for the improvement of the harbor and the promotion of commerce, a perpetual benefit would be conferred upon the whole people.

" We regard this interest in the flats as a sort of marine investment for the benefit of the State, which should be managed with a sole reference to the commercial prosperity of the whole people. Nor is this a partial or local view of the subject. Though these flats do not belong, as property, to the county of Suffolk, any more than to the county of Berkshire, yet it is the prosperity of Boston which has given a value to this property, and contributed to the general prosperity of the State. And though the disposition of these flats which we have indicated might, in the first instance, be more productive to the interest of Boston and its vicinity than to the rest of the Commonwealth, its beneficial effects would soon be realized by the people at large. Boston is not only the political but the commercial capital of the State; and whatever increases her commercial prosperity, confers a direct benefit upon the whole people, by creating a market, and increasing the demand for labor, and for every article that labor can produce. The commercial prosperity of the city increases the amount of taxable property in the State, and gives rise to those moneyed institutions and business transactions from which the State derives its principal revenue. This commercial prosperity also gives an impulse to our manufacturing and mechanical industry, thereby creating a market for agricultural products, not only in our cities, but in every village throughout the State. If the Legislature, to realize a present pecuniary advantage, should dispose of all the flats in which the State has an interest, and should suffer them to be filled, to the ruin of the channel, and commerce should desert the city, the withering effects would soon be felt in the business prosperity of the whole State; and our young men would leave our rugged hills and ungenial climate, to seek in other States that employment which their own denied them. If the Legislature, therefore, look to the permanent welfare of the whole people, they cannot, in our estimation, make a better or wiser disposition of them than to dedicate them to the interest of commerce. The treasure is found in the deep; and let it be so appropriated that that deep may bear upon its surface, and bring to our shores, the more useful treasures of which we may all partake. But though we should regard it as unwise, and unjust to one portion of the community, to grant these flats to an individual or corporation, without consideration, yet we would recommend that a liberal policy be adopted; and if any portion of them can be filled without detriment to the harbor, grants should be made upon terms so favorable as to encourage enterprize, and ensure the completion of the work, that thereby an additional amount of property may be created, to sustain, by taxation and otherwise, the interests of the people.

"We believe that the growing commerce of the city will, within fifty years, require the utmost capacity of the harbor; and that nothing should be filled which is capable, by excavation, of being converted, at a reasonable expense, into wet docks or roadsteads."

Following out this idea, the commissioners propose a line which they say will save to the harbor about 450 acres, that Mr. Carey's line would allow to be filled. They also recommend the excavation of the flats below the proposed line, suggest a system of wet docks, and present a sketch of the same prepared by W. P. Parrott, Esq., engineer.

"The flats in the harbor of Boston seem admirably adapted to the purpose of wet docks. In the first place, they are situated near the centre of business, which cannot be said of the Atlantic Docks in New York. Nor is it necessary to destroy a large amount of valuable land covered with buildings, as was the case at Liverpool and London. With us, the flats, at present, are useless; and, by converting them into wet docks, a large amount of land will be created, suitable for warehouses. Such docks would answer the double purpose of land and water, — giving an additional amount of wharf-room and storehouses, and at the same time affording the largest accommodation for the shipping in the harbor. Besides, that portion of the harbor is somewhat exposed to easterly winds, and the sea wall enclosing the docks would act as a break water, and so protect, not only the ships in the docks, but those in the upper portion of Fore Point Channel. Nor would the advantages be confined to the harbor. By excavating the flats in front of Fore Point Channel, all that portion of the city from India wharf to Summer Street wharf, would be brought directly to deep water, and the value of property in that part of the city would be greatly increased.

"Another advantage resulting from such improvement in this part of the harbor is this: — it would open a more direct communication between our railroads and deep water. The Lowell, Fitchburg, Maine, and Eastern railroads enter the northern part of the city, and can find deep water in that region of Boston or Charlestown, or by the Grand Junction Railroad, of East Boston. But the Old Colony, Worcester, and Providence roads enter the city in the southerly section, and hence would be accommodated by a connection with deep water on Fore Point Channel. The prospective growth of our inland trade, makes it highly important that improvements be made in every part of the harbor, which will facilitate that valuable part of our trade."

In reference to the flats in Mystic River, the Commissioners say,—

"There is another considerable portion of flats in Mystic River, between Malden and Chelsea bridges, a grant of which has been asked by the citizens of Charlestown. This tract contains about one hundred acres. These flats not only belong to the Commonwealth, but their title is embarrassed by no water rights of the riparian owners. By the law of 1641, no proprietor was allowed to cross any creek or channel; and, as there is a channel on each side of the river, and these flats are situated between the channels, they cannot legally be claimed by the shore owners, on either side of the river. The commissioners are inclined to the opinion, that these flats might be filled, and the navigation of the river thereby improved. They were, however, inclined to believe, that the plan proposed, extended too far below Chelsea Bridge into the channel. And they had some apprehension, that confining the flow of the water to the Chelsea shore, might produce an eddy, and cause a deposit on the flats near the navy yard, to the injury of that establishment, and of navigation in that part of the harbor. But if the Legislature, in their wisdom, should see fit to make this grant for sufficient consideration, they should provide that the material to fill the flats to the height of extreme high water, should be taken from the marshes above, between high and low water marks, so that the river should be capable of receiving and discharging as large a quantity of tide water as at present. The materials should be taken under the direction of some skilful person, appointed by the government, who should see that it be

E

taken, not only between high and low water, but at such points, and in such a manner, as to improve the navigation of the river; and that the parts excavated, be so situated as not to be liable to fill up with sediment. The company should also be required to excavate the flats below their embankment to the channel,—and to keep the flats, the channel of the river, and the marshes so excavated, open to a given depth. These precautions appear to the commissioners to be indispensably necessary to the safety of the harbor, and the Legislature would be false to the trust reposed in them, to make a grant without securing the performance of these, or similar duties, in the most ample manner."

They also consider the subject of the flats in the Back Bay. No extracts are made from that part of the report, as those flats are undoubtedly lost for every valuable purpose to the harbor. The Commissioners, however, travel a little out of their way to say,—

"They (the Water Power Company,) have also, by contract or compromise, permitted the reservoir to be abridged to a large extent, by the city of Boston, who seem never to have hesitated to give precedence to the proprietary right of making land for sale, over the commercial value of flats and tide waters to the harbor."

The conclusion is as follows,—

"The commissioners would respectfully recommend to the Legislature, to retain in their own hands, all such portions of these flats as are not imperiously demanded by the present wants of the community. Let not the plea that the flats are wanted for building purposes, or that the harbor is ample to meet the present and future wants of commerce, induce the Legislature to grant to individuals or corporations what, at no distant day, must be required by the public for the accommodation of trade. Nor would it, in our judgment, be wise to surrender these flats, or the guardianship of them, to the city of Boston, or in any other city or town in which they are located. It has been recommended by one commission, to surrender them to the city of Boston,— which, it is said, having the most direct interest, would appropriate them in the wisest manner for the interest of commerce. But we should fear that the interest of Boston would be too direct for a wise disposition of this property. The policy which this city is now pursuing, is filling up south Bay, after every board of commissioners has reported that such a course would be ruinous to certain portions of the harbor, leads to the apprehension, that she might not prove the best guardian of the commercial interests of the State.

"If these flats were granted to any of these cities, to be appropriated for the public good, there would be great danger that local considerations would control the manner of their disposal. The question of their disposition would soon become a matter of party contest, and there would be danger that present interest would prevail over public considerations, and that grants of an impolitic character would be made. Grants, looking more to immediate income, than to future growth,—more to private than to public considerations,—more to local advantage, than to the general welfare.

"These flats being the property of the whole people,—and the members of the Legislature coming from all parts of the Commonwealth, and knowing the wishes of their constituents,—we know of no body so well qualified to exercise a wise guardianship over this great interest as the General Court. The property is in their hands; and there we may safely trust it; knowing that in them, we have a tribunal as independent and impartial as the lot of humanity will admit."

This report was referred to the Joint Standing Committee of the Legislature, on Mercantile Affairs and Insurance, of which the Hon. Benjamin Seaver, present mayor of the city, was chairman.

The following extracts, made from their report, in Senate, April 26, 1850, will show that the views of the Commissioners were severely criticized, and particular attention is called to the manner in which the unjust imputation of the Commissioners upon the city of Boston is answered,—

"The commissioners, if we rightly understand them, take the ground, that (with certain exceptions, arising mainly out of the ordinance of 1641, and the Constitution of the United States,) the Commonwealth has the absolute title to the flats, both the property and every beneficial use, as fully as the allodial title a citizen has to his farm. Their reasoning is this: The king held the fee in lands, under tide waters, in trust, for the use of his subjects; and Parliament, which represents the subjects, had the control of this trust and use; that the Commonwealth succeeds to the rights of both the Crown and Parliament, and the trust is, therefore, merged in the fee, and the title becomes absolute. We understand their opinion, therefore, to be, that the title of the State to the flats is the same, as respects the degree and kind of property, with that which it holds in the State House yard, the arsenal lands, and in its wild lands in Maine ; that they are property, to be sold, at the discretion of the Legislature, and the proceeds put into the treasury, the purchaser, if not especially restricted, gaining the right to fill up and build upon them, except, perhaps, as against certain private rights of riparian proprietors.

"This is matter of great consequence ; for it should be borne in mind, that the same rule applies to channels, and the deep sea, within county lines, as to the flats. We are not ready to acquiesce in this result, and the reasoning upon which it rests seems to us too technical. By the law of all civilized Europe, before the feudal system obtained in England, there was no such thing as property in tide waters. Tide waters were *res omnium*, that is, they were for the common use, like air and light. If the sea receded, or by the operation of natural or artificial means, the sea ceased to flow in certain spaces, the land under the water would, doubtless go to the abutters, by accretion, or alluvion. In England, the fiction of a fee in the Crown, and the control of the trust in Parliament, we understand to have been a mode, suited to the times and the genius of the feudal law, for insuring to the State the control over tide waters. The Commonwealth succeeds to this right of control. By its sovereign authority, for the benefit of the public, it regulates the use of tide waters, and, any title it may have in lands under them is only incidental to the tide waters, and held for the reason, that control over the land is necessary to the control of the sea above it. The property the State has in the channels and harbors, is evidently held only upon reasons of public policy, all depending upon, and arising out of the fact, that they are under tide waters. This is not property that the State has purchased, or holds by conquest, as it holds its wild lands, and its State House, and arsenal yards. Its right is simply a rule of law, depending upon reasons of State, and when the reason ceases, the rule should cease also. Whatever may occur to its public lands, by natural or artificial means, the property remains unaffected. But, if the sea should entirely recede from a bay or basin, and the land under it should gradually change to marsh, and then to upland, is it supposed that the State would own this land, in its new condition, as its absolute property ? Does the State, at this moment, own all the lands, now marsh or uplands, which it ever held, as channels, or below the ordinance line, from which the sea has receded, since the settlement of Massachusetts ? If the commissioners' argument is sound, whenever a channel, within one hundred rods of high water mark, fills up, so as to become part of the flats, the title to it is not in the riparian proprietor, but in the State. How far the same rule should apply, when the sea is shut out by artificial means from channels, or flats below the ordinance line, we are not required to say. But we express our doubt, whether the Commonwealth can disregard the reason upon which its title rests, and sell channels and harbors to be used for other purposes, putting the full value of an absolute title into its treasury. The novelty of the doctrine now set up,—the fact, that no instance is known in any country, where the sovereign power has undertaken to *sell* this species of property, and the universal practice of this Commonwealth, from our earliest history, must be regarded as important considerations in the discussion of such a question. The fact of the grant by the ordinance of 1641, of the flats before men's estates; the fact, that the Legislature has constantly granted to proprietors the right to extend wharves, without charge ; the various acts in relation to the harbors in the State, all show conclusively, that the policy of the Commonwealth has been entirely adverse to the exercise of any such extreme right as that now set up.

" Your committee believe, that the exercise of any such doctrine is as inexpedient as it is unjust. The *whole* State is interested in the harbors of the Commonwealth. If the idea is to be entertained and acted upon, that the flats in the various harbors are vendible property, liable to be put into the market, sold, and the proceeds put into the treasury of the State, it will tend to injure the harbors, by throwing the flats into the hands of speculators, and thus introduce a new and dangerous element into the policy of the State. Your committee believe, that the flats in *all* the harbors of the State should be used only for the benefit of those harbors. They should be granted, not for private benefit, not for public economical result, but strictly for the benefit of the harbors, where they are situated. Whenever a petition is presented for leave to occupy them, the single question should be, *as it always has been*,—will the grant benefit the harbor ? or,—will the increased facilities, which will be given to commerce and commercial enterprise, *compensate* for any slight detriment of the harbor ? There may be great public enterprises and improvements to carry out, for which it will be necessary to grant large portions of flats. In such cases, if individuals or corporations are to be benefited, the State may stipulate, that, as a consideration for the grant, they shall make certain other improvements in the same harbor. In other words, the flats in each and every harbor of the State should be devoted entirely to the benefit and improvement of that particular harbor.

" The city of Boston was represented before the committee, by the city solicitor, and a committee of the city council. Strong exceptions were taken to those expressions, in the report of the commissioners, which refer to the conduct of the city of Boston, in relation to the flats in Boston harbor. Thus, the commissioners, on page 45, allude to that city as seeming ' never to have hesitated to give preference, to the proprietary right of making land for sale, over the commercial value of flats and tide waters to the harbor.' Again, on page 46, ' the policy which the city is now pursuing in filling up South Bay, after every board of commissioners has reported, that such a course would be ruinous to certain portions of the harbor, leads to the apprehension, that she might not prove the best guardian of the commercial interests of the State.

" In regard to the remark first above quoted, the counsel for the city denied that there was any evidence, whatever, furnished by the commissioners, to sustain it, nor was there any such evidence in existence. He declared it to be without evidence and without foundation, and a gratuitous imputation upon a city which has a deeper interest than any other portion of the State can have in preserving Boston Harbor.

" In regard to filling up South Bay, the facts appear to be these :—In the report of Messrs. Hayward and Lincoln, made in 1846, they state the area of South Bay to be 345 acres. This area is about 75 or 80 acres larger than formerly, the bordering marsh land having been excavated, for the purpose of filling up the South Cove and other neighboring flats. The city of Boston have a large tract of marsh land, east of Harrison Avenue, which could not be suitably improved without building a sea wall at great expense. From the condition of this land, its liability to become a nuisance and source of filth in that part of the city, and from the necessity of making more extensive arrangements for a more effective drainage, the city entered into a very expensive contract to build a sea-wall, and fill about sixty-nine acres of the flats which belong to the city, by a title as good as any title in the Commonwealth. Nor was this operation commenced in the dark. In the year 1847, the city petitioned the Legislature for leave to construct a railroad from the Providence Railroad to these flats for this very purpose, and an act was passed for that purpose. (Act of 1847, chapter 250.) Failing to make an arrangement with the Providence Railroad Company, the city then petitioned for leave to construct a railroad from the Old Colony Railroad across South Bay for the same purpose. This was strenuously resisted by the city of Roxbury, on account of the obstruction to navigation, but was granted after a full hearing on the merits, and the act was passed and the bridge built. (Act of 1848, chapter 37.) This subject, in one form or another, has been repeatedly before the Legislature, or some of the committees, and no objection has ever been made to the project, but it has been regarded as a great public improvement. And when it is remembered, that the city are only filling up the flats which belong to it by a perfect title ; that they are doing this, not as a private speculation, but as great public improvement demanded by a due regard to the health and prosperity of the city ; that the Legislature

APPENDIX. 39

have sanctioned the work by two special acts, and that, after these flats are filled, South Bay will have a larger area than before South Cove was filled up, your committee do not see any foundation for the remarks made by the commissioners."

The Legislative Committee obtained the opinion of Mr. James Hayward, civil engineer, and a member of two of the previous boards of Commissioners, which is attached to their report. Mr. Hayward considers it " above all things desirable that the main body of these (the South Boston,) flats should be devoted to a system of tidal basins, wet docks, warehouses, and other facilities for conducting the commerce of this port, which the increasing business of this country is certainly soon to demand, and for which the locality in question is remarkably well adapted." He, however, differs entirely from the Commissioners, in regard to the excavation of the flats, and advocates the erection and maintenance of a seawall on the east side of Fore Point Channel,—

" This entire section of the harbor, presenting a front of one mile in length, is directly exposed to the southeast winds, which have been the most destructive to which the harbor is ever exposed. It would be a great boon to the owners of that property, and, indirectly, to that section of the city, to have the whole line of wharves—from the free bridge down to India wharf—perfectly protected from all winds,—as it would be by this improvement. Fore Point channel would then be a complete *tidal basin*, in every particular as good as that of the Atlantic Dock, in the port of New York, which has been recently built at a great expense. It will, when built round, according to the design, have fifty per cent. more water front than the Atlantic Basin, and about twenty-five per cent. greater area of water surface, and all this exclusive of the slips on the sides of this channel. It may be made to accommodate a greater number of vessels, than the New York basin, and these vessels would be as perfectly protected. The area of this channel, between the free bridge and its mouth, is just equal to the two great basins,—the *import* and *export* basins, of the West India Docks in London. There is not a wharf on that channel which would not be increased in value by carrying out these improvements. On the contrary, excavating these flats, as proposed by the late commissioners, will totally destroy Fore Point Channel. The current in this channel would entirely cease, and the water in front of all the wharves, from Hobbs' wharf to

Long wharf, would be either a gentle eddy, or nearly a dead pool; and it would be found, that this channel and the docks, along and between these wharves, would fill up faster than they ever have before.

"That the excavation of these flats would be likely to cause Fore Point channel to fill up, and that a sea-wall on the eastern side of that channel would tend to avert that evil, even the report of the late commissioners furnishes some *incidental evidence*. It informs us, that 'some of the most intelligent and practical of those who had given depositions in favor of a sea-wall on the eastern side of this channel, found their opinion of its utility upon the apprehension, that the great volume of water from South Bay might cut a new channel through the flats to the main ship channel, *and so leave Fore Point Channel to fill up.*' The *report* adds, that 'much of this testimony would be materially modified by the present state of things, relative to the filling up of South Bay.' This is, probably, an *inference* of the commissioners; but there must be some mistake, either of principle or of fact. If these deponents apprehended that the refluent waters from South Bay might wear a new channel across the South Boston flats, and thus deprive Fore Point Channel of the scouring agency of these waters, and recommended the erection of a sea-wall to force these waters to pass through this channel, and thus to avert the calamity, I should not feel quite at liberty to *infer*, that these 'intelligent and practical' gentlemen would change their minds as to the importance of a *scour* for this channel, because the quantity of water, available for this purpose, was liable to be considerably diminished. If it is to be apprehended, that the water from South Bay may, in a course of years, wear a new channel through the flats, and thus destroy Fore Point Channel, it is quite obvious, that excavating the flats, which are the only barrier against such action of the water, must hasten the apprehended catastrophe. And I find it not easy to believe, that these intelligent witnesses would doubt, that the proposed sea-wall, or some equivalent structure, would be the proper protection to this channel, with a smaller quantity of water as well as with a larger.

"But the greatest evil *likely*, and I think I may say, *certain*, to result from the excavation of this great body of flats,—is *the gradual destruction of the main channel of the harbor*. Serious evils are likely to follow from the encroachments which have been made on the east side of this channel, by bringing so far forward into deep water, the East Boston wharves. Its tendency is to create a change in the main channel, by wearing off on the south side, just below the mouth of Fore Point Channel, and causing it to shoal in front of the lower wharves in East Boston. The excavation of the flats would, inevitably, increase this evil; whereas, the tendency of the pier which the commissioners of 1846, proposed to be erected along the margin of this channel, would be, to arrest this process of deterioration, before the evil shall become irremediable."

Mr. Hayward points out certain errors in the statement of of the commissioners, as follows, viz.,—

"It is quite manifest, that the sources of information on which the late commissioners have relied, are, in many instances, far from being authentic. They have fallen into a mistake with respect to the amount of tide-water which has been excluded by filling up the flats in and about the city. The report goes on to particularize: '*Boston proper*, which originally contained less than 1,000 acres, now contains more than 3,000 acres. This increase of more than 2,000 acres, has all been made by encroachments upon tide-water. In addition to this, the mill-dam cut off 700 or 800 acres more,—to this may be added the large quantity of land made at Cambridge, Charlestown, Chelsea, and East Boston. Here we have an area of several thousand acres which are forever lost to the harbor.' This certainly looks appalling, but it is mostly imagination. Boston proper, instead of containing 'more than 3,000 acres' above high-water mark, contains, at this moment, less than half that area. This correction reduces, very essentially, the 'increase which has been made by encroachments upon tide-water.' The amount cut off by the mill-dam is, I believe, not over-stated. But the material for the 'large quantity of land,' said to be, made in Cambridge,—that made on the south and west side of Charlestown, and a large amount on the west and northwest, as well as on the south sides of Boston proper, and no inconsiderable amount at East Boston and South Boston, has been taken from the marshes and flats, between high and low watermarks, in the rivers and bays above the harbor, which has enlarged these estuaries to that amount, and thus, has been a benefit, rather than a detriment, to the harbor channels. The principal exception to this beneficial effect is, that too much of this material was taken from South Bay instead of being taken from the larger estuaries above the harbor."

And says in reference to the change in the current between Boston and East Boston,—

"The main cause of this change in the current between Boston and East Boston, particularly at ebb tide, is undoubtedly the extension of the wharves at East Boston. It was, without doubt, a great mistake to allow the wharves on that island to project so far into the main channel. It was considered, by the harbor commissioners of 1835, to be a misfortune that the passage for the tide could not be widened on that side, without disturbing then existing *improvements ;* but further encroachment has been since made upon the main channel on that side.

"I have no doubt that, in the course of the next generation, the commerce of Boston will be quadrupled. And it is with reference to its future wants, and the desirableness, at all times, —of affording the utmost facilities for doing this business,—of laying upon it the fewest possible burdens,—that I am obliged to differ from the commissioners as to their general views of the harbor, and the details which are mainly contemplated in their report. The measures which are definitely recommended, by the commissioners, to be pursued by the present generation, are such as will not only take from the premises in question those characteristics which constitute their principal value in relation to the expected wants of commerce at this port,—but they will really put at hazard the most important feature of the present harbor,—the main channel between the city and Fort Independence.

"It is, without doubt, a great error to suppose that the principal want of commerce at this port is *anchorage ground.* And it would be a fatal mistake to excavate those flats to a depth of twelve feet below low-water mark, *with the idea of benefiting commerce,*—to say nothing of the expense of it ; which will be for the whole five hundred acres, several millions of dollars."

The eighth commission, consisting of Simon Greenleaf, Joel Giles and Ezra Lincoln, Jr., Esquires, was appointed under authority of resolves of the Legislature, approved May 3, 1850.

This commission was authorized to define upon a plan or plans, such lines as they shall think expedient to establish, beyond which no wharves shall be extended into and over the tide waters of the Commonwealth, on the flats on the easterly side of Fore Point channel, and northerly shore of South Boston.

Also to examine if any alterations in the lines and channels of South Bay, or any part of Fore Point Channel, be necessary to preseve the depth of water, or prevent the formation of shoals, and bars thereon.

Also to make inquiries respecting the flats in the Back Bay, and report what measures can be taken for the improvement of the same. As it is not supposed that any further injury to the harbor of Boston can be occasioned by the improvement of flats from which the tide-water is now excluded, no extracts will be made from their report referring to that subject.

The commissioners were also authorized to obtain the advice and assistance of the attorney-general of the Commonwealth, upon any legal points or questions that might be involved in the examination of the several subjects referred to them.

The well known ability of the commissioners, and the attention paid by them to the legal merits of the case, gives weight to their opinion and entitles it to particular consideration. The report, from which the following extracts have been made, is dated March 22, 1851.

" 1. The title of the Commonwealth [to the flats in question] may be deduced in the first place from the right of *eminent domain*, which is an inherent attribute of sovereignty. It is the paramount right, which every sovereign state possesses, of disposing of all the property within its jurisdiction, as the safety and well being of the whole may require. The right of determining the existence and extent of the public exigencies must rest with those to whom the exercise of sovereign power is entrusted. Under our constitution, all public property is, in the first instance, entrusted by the people to the Legislature, to be administered and disposed of for the good of the whole. This trust is in its nature discretionary. The Legislature must of necessity be the sole judge of the time, manner and circumstances, in and under which the public property shall be applied, or private property be taken, for public uses. And it is not to be supposed that the public functionaries will be regardless of their duty, or incapable of performing it. Against hasty or unwise legislation, our constitution has provided no security but the veto of the executive, and the interest, wisdom and justice of the legislative body, and its relations with its constituents. If, in the exercise of this right of eminent domain, private property is taken, or, which is the same thing, its value is directly impaired, the State is bound to make adequate compensation, upon principles of natural justice, explicitly recognized in the constitution.

" It is universally admitted to be the duty of every government to promote the public convenience, and the interests both of agriculture, and of trade and commerce; and consequently, to provide not only public commons and highways, but common harbors and landing places for these puposes. The right of travel and navigation, in the pursuit of lawful business, is the *jus publicum*, or right of all men, subject to which, as modified and limited in its exercise by the sovereign power, all real property is holden.

"The commissioners, therefore, conceive it to be clear, that this Commonwealth has the right, in the exercise of its eminent domain, to define the territorial limits beyond which no riparian proprietor of lands shall obstruct the free flow of navigable waters, or impede the passage of any vessel or property, water-borne; and the right to take any measures, in its discretion, to protect its harbors from injury, and to render them safe and commodious for navigation by all the citizens.

"2. There is, in the second place, a title in the Commonwealth, to what is termed 'the soil of the sea,' that is, to the land covered by tide-waters, within its territorial limits.

"This title may be deduced from general principles of national law. Writers of acknowledged authority on this subject agree, that 'everything, susceptible of property, belongs to the nation that possesses the country, and as forming the entire mass of its wealth,' and 'that when a nation takes possession of a country, everything that is not divided among its members remains common to the whole nation, and is called *public wealth*. The nation, in monarchies, is represented, in regard to its property, by 'the crown,' which holds the national domains in trust; in this country the title to such property is vested in the State or people, the power of disposal being in the legislative body. And as the land covered by the sea is a thing in its nature susceptible of property, this State, as soon as it became a sovereign power, became the owner of all the lands within its territorial limits, which had not already become the property of private persons; including, of course, the flats in question.

"3. This title may also be deduced from the crown of England, by actual conveyances. That the title to the soil of the sea was vested in the crown at the time of the first settlement of this country, is now too well settled to admit of question. It is so laid down by that great jurist, Lord Hale, in his treatise *De Jure Maris*, beyond which no authority need be cited; and this doctrine has uniformly been admitted in this country, in all our judicial tribunals, without dispute.

"King James I., having this title, in the year 1620, granted to the Plymouth Company 'all that part of America,' between the fortieth and forty-eighth degrees of north latitude; including not only the 'firm lands,' but also the 'soils, grounds, *havens, ports*, rivers and waters' therein, and the islands on the coast. In 1627, the Plymouth Company conveyed to Sir Henry Rosewell and others, 'all that part of New England' extending from three miles northward of Merrimack river to three miles southward of the southernmost part of Massachusetts Bay; with the same particular enumeration of the soils, grounds, *havens, ports*, islands, &c. This charter was confirmed by letters patent of King Charles I., in 1628; and though these letters were unjustly vacated by chancery in 1684, yet the chartered rights of the Massachusetts Company were restored, and the Province of Massachusetts constituted, by a subsequent charter, granted Oct. 7, 1691, by William and Mary. Under this charter, the Province of Massachusetts held all the teritorial rights and titles now in question, down to the period of the revolution, at which time they passed to the Commonwealth. This property is thus vested in the State, for the general benefit of the people; subject to be managed, ordered and disposed of, like other public property, as the Legislature in its wisdom may deem most conducive to the good of the whole. The commissioners are unable to find any practical distinction between one kind of public property and another, so far as regards the right of legislative disposal. Should the Legislature be inveigled into an unwise grant to individuals, either of property or of corporate franchises or powers, the grant must stand upon the same footing with grants of private property or easements by private persons. If the grant amounts to the alienation of any attribute of sovereignty, entrusted to the legislative body for purposes of government, it is merely void for want of authority in the Legislature to make the grant. And if, being within the powers entrusted to the Legislature, any grant has been obtained by fraud and imposition, it may for that cause be set aside in the courts of law.

"It was argued, with much ingenuity and learning, before the commissioners, that the State was entitled to the soil under tide water only as an incident to the waters themselves; that these were common property, or *res omnium;* and that when the waters receded, or were shut out, the title of the sovereign receded also, and was excluded; and hence it was inferred, that the State could have no absolute title to the soil under tide waters, nor to the lands from which those waters are excluded, whether by natural causes, or by artificial dams and embankments, made by public authority. This reasoning, though universal in its terms, was especially applied to the lands within the Receiving Basin of the Boston and Roxbury Mill Dam, in Back Bay.

"In regard to lands, gained from the sea by alluvion, or imperceptible and gradual accretion, by the natural and ordinary action of the waters, it is universally admitted that they belong to the riparian proprietor. It is equally clear, that the losses of soil, occasioned in like manner, are to be borne by the proprietor alone. He takes the chances both of loss and of gain. But this rule is founded, not upon the notion of any reliction or extinguishment of the title of the State, as depending on tide waters, or any act of the State; but on the principle that such imperceptible accessions are the natural growth of the land to which they are attached, as the growth of a tree belongs to the tree; and on the maxim of right, which gives the profits and advantages of a thing to him who is exposed to suffer its damages and its losses. In like manner, and on the same principle, what is gained from the flats or bank, by similar gradual action of the waters, is gained to the state owning the soil of the sea.

" But it is not easy to perceive any necessary connection between the right to control tide waters, and the title to the soil over which they flow; nor any dependence of the one upon the other. The tide waters are nothing more than a common highway, over which the right of passage, which is common to all, is not yet restricted to particular lines and limits; and such the whole territory of the State would be, if no private citizen owned any portion of it in severalty.

" This universal right of passage and travel, whether on land or water, is regulated and controlled by the State, in virtue of its right of government, as an attribute of sovereignty, and not in virtue of any proprietorship in the soil. On the upland, where the State owns nothing, the land being held by private persons, this right of control, in the making, altering and regulating of highways, remains nevertheless in the State, in full and unimpaired amplitude and vigor; it would also remain, to the same extent, in regard to the control of the tide-waters, if the State owned nothing in the soil under them. Its title to this soil, as we have already seen, is derived from other sources; by virtue of which it owns all the lands within its bounds, whether under water or above water, which it has not granted away. Such grant, if any there be, may always readily be shown, by the production or other proof of the charter, resolve or deed, or by evidence of ancient and exclusive possession, from which a charter or grant may be presumed.

" It may be added, that the title of the State, as absolute owner of all the land covered by water, lying below low-water mark, or more than one hundred rods from high-water mark, though it has not been directly adjudicated upon, to the knowledge of the commissioners, has been several times distinctly recognized by the Supreme Judicial Court, as an unquestioned title, in reference to the ground within the Receiving Basin of the Boston and Roxbury Mill Corporation. (See 12 Pickering's Reports, 476; 23 Pickering's Reports, 391.)

" The fallacy of the reasoning which makes the title of the State to the land in question depend on its control of the tide waters, is supposed to arise from not distinguishing between things which are the common property of all men, without regard to national character, being in their nature incapable of separate possession; of which the air, and light, and the high seas are examples; and those things which are capable of separate possession, and are the property of the State, subject to its absolute control for the common good; among which are the sea near its coast, the banks of the sea, and the ports and harbors within its territorial limits.

"The commissioners, while they perceive no limit to the power of the Legislature to manage and dispose of these public lands, as well as any other public property, except such limit as its own good judgment and discretion may prescribe, are nevertheless of opinion that the preservation of our harbors is an important public trust, which ought always to be kept in view in disposing of the flats therein; especially when it is considered that the interest of private individuals leads to continual encroachments on the tide waters, by extending their wharves and embankments.

"II. Such being the general title of the Commonwealth, the next inquiry is, as to the titles of private citizens and corporations to any lands within the original bounds of the harbor.

"The title of the Plymouth Company, as derived from the crown of England, originally covered all the land below highwater mark. But, by the *Colonial Ordinance of* 1641, the proprietor of the land adjoining tide waters, became entitled to the land ' to the low-water mark, where the sea doth not ebb above a hundred rods, and not more wheresoever it ebbs further; provided, that such proprietor shall not by this liberty have power to stop or hinder the passage of boats or other vessels, in or through any sea, creeks or coves, to other men's houses or lands.' This ordinance is the source and foundation of all the right which riparian proprietors have to the flats below their respective lands. The extent of the right has not been fully and completely defined by any judicial decision, to the knowledge of the commissioners; but it has been adjudged, that any natural creek, in which the tide ebbed and flowed, and from which it did not ebb at the times when from natural causes, it ebbed the lowest, would constitute the ulterior boundary of the flats. It has also been held, that by force of this ordinance, the riparian proprietor has a fee in the soil of the flats, to the extent therein described, as parcel of and incident to his upland; but that he holds it only *sub modo*, limited and qualified by the proviso therein contained; that he may build a wharf or other permanent structure upon it, or he may enclose it with rows of piles, so as to exclude other persons from it; but that he is restricted from making such a use of it, as would impair the public right of passing over the water in boats or other vessels to other men's houses or lands; it being the intention of the ordinance, to reserve a free passage over the water in such places, ' to other men's houses and lands,' in the same manner as it existed before the public property in the shore was transferred.

"The right of the proprietor to the use of the flats being thus held, subject to the paramount public right of passage over them when covered with water, the question has been raised, whether it is competent for the Legislature to prescribe the method of using this public right of passage, and to fix a limit, beyond which no wharf or other obstruction shall be erected to impair it, without the payment of any damages to the owner of the flats. In the solution of this question, it is to be considered, that the right of way, intended to be preserved by the ordinance, is, from its nature, a public, and not a private way ; it is not a way restricted to the houses or lands of the adjacent or any other particular class of proprietors ; but it is a way to ' other men's,' namely, all other men's, estates, anywhere. Such ways it is the duty of every government to provide, when requisite for the convenience of its citizens ; and the legislative act by which such convenient way or passage is secured, whether it be in the form of a statute or a resolve, and whether general or particular, is conceived to be merely the ordinary exercise of sovereign power, in the regular course of good government. And the establishment of the commissioners' or harbor line, so called, beyond which no wharf shall be extended, is nothing else than a legislative act, defining the limits and boundary, and securing the safety, of a public highway for navigation, which it is perfectly competent for the Legislature to do. If, then, the ordinance of 1641, with its proviso, is to be expounded as a grant of the flats, subject to the perpetual public easement and servitude of such right of way, the act of the Legislature, in defining the limits and boundaries, and securing the safety of such way, would not seem to subject the Commonwealth to the payment of damages to the owner of the flats ; for, in that case, nothing would be taken from him for public use which he ever owned. The case may, in this view, be likened to any grant of land by the State subject to the location of a road over it, in such manner as the State might afterwards determine ; or the grant of a township of land, subject to the public use of its navigable waters. But if the ordinance, with its proviso, is to be expounded as a grant of the flats upon condition that the grantee shall not erect any obstruction thereon to the free passage of boats and vessels, then the act of the Legislature, in establishing the extreme limit of any solid embankment, or, in other words, in defining the harbor line, may be regarded as an exercise of the right of eminent domain, taking private property for public use ; in which case, the owner of the land thus taken would be entitled to the payment, by the Commonwealth, of such damages, as he may thereby have sustained. In either case, the right of the Legislature to establish such line is beyond question.

"Which of these is the true interpretation of the ordinance, is

APPENDIX.

a question of no inconsiderable difficulty. And as it is understood to be involved in a case now under advisement in the Supreme Judicial Court, the commissioners deem it proper to await its decision by that tribunal."

In considering the lines to be established upon South Boston flats, they say,—

"These flats contain about five hundred and fifty acres, between the high and low-water lines. About two hundred acres, fronting northeasterly on the main channel, and northwesterly on Fore Point Channel, are below the line of riparian proprietorship, and belong to the State. The average depth of high water upon these flats is about nine feet. When covered with water, they form part of the roadstead of Boston harbor, and afford harbor-room and anchorage, upon their margins, for coasters and vessels of light draught; when bare, these flats are a source of unwholesome nuisances, and they prevent water access to the entire northern shore of South Boston, and effectually separate that important section of the city from its main centres of business. The magnitude of these inconveniences will go on increasing with the population and business of the city. A wise forecast, therefore, clearly requires a division and appropriation of these flats to the uses of the harbor and the shore, respectively, according to their present and prospective exigencies.

"The value of the whole of South Boston will be greatly enhanced by building out its northern shore, and excavating the margins of the channels, until good wharf and dock accommodations are obtained, and by making a new and broad avenue, running from the foot of Summer street, nearly parallel with West Broadway, to the vicinity of the city institutions. It is evident to the commissioners, that some such improvements will certainly be made, at no distant day, for they are wanted by the public. The question is, how can these exigencies be satisfied without injury to the harbor? To answer this question, it must be observed, that there are but two places, in the main channel of the harbor, where apparently much danger is to be apprehended from shoaling, or a change of currents. The first, and most important of these, is at the Narrows, in the lower harbor. Matthew Hunt, a pilot of forty years' experience, stated to the commissioners, that the depth of water in the Narrows has materially lessened within the period of his observation; and, if the changes now taking place there shall go on as fast for twenty years more, that channel will be destroyed for large vessels; that the spit on the easterly end of Gallop's Island is making out into the channel, and already turns much of the flood tide from the Narrows, through a side channel, into Nantasket Roads, in a direction south of Long Island, and around into Hingham harbor. He further stated, that the channel through the Narrows, which is the only ship channel for large vessels, at all times safe and practicable, into and out of the harbor, is not much over six hundred feet wide, from ten feet soundings on one margin to ten feet soundings on the other; and at mean low water, the least depth is twenty five or six feet. Upon the preservation of this narrow channel, therefore, depends the safety and value of Boston harbor, and the millions of local property in its vicinity. But, in the opinion of the commissioners, these unfavorable changes which are going on in the Narrows, are owing to local causes, which are mainly the extension and enlargement of the *spits* on the east end of Gallop's Island, the southwest side of Lovell's Island, and the west end of the Great Brewster. The present and ultimate effects of these increasing spits upon the Narrows deserve the immediate and serious attention of the Legislature and of Congress; and prompt measures should be adopted by Congress and by the State, to prevent the further washing away of the islands in the lower harbor. This must be done, in a great measure, by walling them around on the seaward side, and by placing heavy stone ballast upon their beaches; and such material portions of the islands as cannot certainly be preserved while remaining private property, should at once be purchased by the State, or by the United States, for the purpose of being secured against further destruction.

"As, however, the Narrows are far down the lower harbor, and nearly five miles from the South Boston flats, the commissioners, after maturely weighing all the considerations pertinent to the case, cannot perceive any reasonable probability that the establishment of the harbor lines, hereinafter described and recommended, will produce any injurious effects upon that critical part of the main ship channel.

"The other important point in the harbor channel, to which the attention of the commissioners has been specially directed, is called the Upper Middle, which is a shoal of sticky Mud in the main channel, lying off the lower end of the South Boston flats, and about equidistant from Castle Island on the southeast, and Governor's Island on the northeast, and just below where the Glades Channel, which is the deepest, though narrow and crooked, branches off to the north of Governor's Island. This shoal seems to be of the nature of a bar, formed by the flood tide in coming up between the two islands above-named; and the Lower Middle may have been formed in a similar manner, by the ebb tide passing down between the same islands.

"A comparison of charts and soundings, of successive dates, does not indicate so much recent shoaling upon the Upper Middle, as the testimony of living witnesses tends to prove. It was stated to the commissioners, by persons who have long observed the changes taking place in the harbor, that the water has shoaled, upon the Upper Middle, more than three feet within the last twenty years. It is now eighteen feet deep there, at mean low water. But whether the water has shoaled there within that period, or whether ships are now built of a larger draught than formerly, it is but too evident that large vessels frequently touch in passing the Upper Middle, and not unfrequently they are obliged to wait for a half or a full tide, before attempting to pass at all. It becomes, therefore, quite material to determine what effect the filling up of any considerable portion of the South Boston flats will have upon this part of the channel.

"Nothing is more difficult than to foresee, with certainty, the ultimate result of any specific alterations in irregular channels, like those of Boston harbor, for the reason that the proximate effects of such alterations become, in turn, themselves the causes of other effects, and so on to infinity, giving rise to a series of casual relations which no scientific formula can grasp and resolve."

In reference to the lines in South Bay, the Commissioners say,—

"The existing harbor line on the east side of the bay, above the South Boston old bridge, runs parallel with Dorchester turnpike, and touches the margin of the deep channel at two points. It was strongly urged upon the commissioners, to recommend an alteration in this line, by advancing it further into the bay, and without regard to the only existing deep channel; requiring, however, that a new channel should be excavated by the riparian owners, before they should fill up the old one; but, after having carefully considered the proposed alteration, in all its bearings upon the public rights, and the interests of navigation, the commissioners are decidedly and unanimously of the opinion that it is inexpedient and unnecessary. The reasons in favor of it are private and inconsiderable, while those against it are public and weighty. South Bay is quite enough contracted by the harbor lines as now established.

"No harbor lines have yet been drawn or established around the southern or upper end of the bay; and the commissioners, though not authorized to draw such lines, cannot omit this opportunity of expressing their opinion of the great importance of immediately extending the harbor line entirely around this bay; and, in completing the harbor line around the bay, the largest tidal area which the State is entitled to retain, or is willing to pay for retaining, should be secured; for upon this scouring basin depends entirely the security and value of Fore Point Channel, with its long line of wharves and docks on either side, down to the main channel of the harbor.

* * * * * *

"The flats in Boston harbor, including its bays and rivers, in which the Commonwealth has a valuable interest, are quite extensive; and the disposition which shall be made of them, whether by keeping them open or filling them up, is a matter of the greatest consequence to the conservation of the harbor, and the interests of navigation; and it may therefore be thought expedient, by the Legislature, to vest the disposition and administration of the public rights in these flats, in some permanent board of trustees or commissioners, who can devise and see to the faithful execution of some general, safe and beneficial plan for the best improvement of these flats, within the limitations and lines which may be established by the Legislature, charging all the expenses of such board upon the proceeds of the flats, which should be so improved, or disposed of, as to remunerate the State for all past or future expenses in regard to the preservation and improvement of Boston harbor. And the commissioners, guided by the experience of other governments upon similar subjects, propose to report a project or bill, " for carrying out the purposes above indicated; and for the full and final execution of their commission, further time is respectfully requested."

By the Act of 1851, chapter 254, the line of the harbor between Battery and Gray's wharves was more accurately defined.

Further time was given to the Commissioners by the resolve of 1851, chapter 80, for the "full and final execution of their commission." On the twenty-fourth of May, 1851, Governor Boutwell vetoed " an Act to authorize the Boston Wharf Company to complete and maintain their wharf." The concluding sentence of the veto message leads to the inference that the Governor was influenced more by the views of the Board of Commissioners, of which he had been a member, than by an investigation of the subject at that time. It is as follows, viz. :

"I need not say that these objections have been prepared without proper opportunities for examination, and may contain errors of fact in regard to certain points which I have presented; but these errors, if shown to exist, will not diminish my confidence in the justice of the conclusion to which I have arrived."

Under the same date, "an Act to establish the Eastern Avenue Corporation," was returned to the Senate by the Governor, with a brief statement of objections, concluding thus:

" It is likely that another avenue to South Boston may, at some future time, be constructed ; but it should have regard to the rights of individuals, the rights of the Commonwealth, and, above all, *to the safety of the harbor.* The bill to which I have made these objections, appears to me to be essentially defective in all these particulars."

The final report of the Commissioners is dated March 11, 1852 ; a large part of it is devoted to an examination of the rights and interests of the Commonwealth, in the flats in Back Bay, and to a consideration of the plans for the improvement of the same.

They also recommend the establishment of a State Commission upon Boston Harbor, and its tributary waters.

A part of the duties proposed for the said Board of permanent Commissioners, is " to watch the effect upon the harbor, of any and all improvements and alterations upon the shore, and within the harbor lines, and of the action of storms upon the islands and channels in the bay, and report the same to the Legislature, for their action, or application to Congress in reference thereto."

In reference to the line of riparian ownership, they say,—

" Some decisions founded on this ordinance seem, on first examination, to establish the principle, that this *propriety* in flats belonging to the land adjoining, though it be but a *liberty* to exclude trespassers, qualified in favor of sea travel, authorizes the riparian proprietors to take exclusive possession of such flats, and forever exclude the sea therefrom, to the extent of low-water mark, when from natural causes it ebbs the lowest, or one hundred rods from the marsh banks, in all the creeks, coves and other places about and upon salt water, where the sea ebbs and flows, in Boston harbor and its tributary waters. If such be the settled construction of the ordinance, then it is in the power of riparian owners, by cutting off and filling up the heads, channels and tidal-ways of such creeks, coves, and other places, to complete, what they have already begun, a serious and irreparable injury to the harbor, and the state and national interests connected therewith.

" It is, however, the opinion of the commissioners, that in all such places, at full sea, there is a public right of way for water passage, even up to the marsh bank, or high water mark ; and that the State has the right to insist, for the safety of the harbor, that the tide shall not be excluded from its natural and ancient channels, and that this right of water-way shall not be impaired by riparian owners, without leave first being obtained in legislative form.

" In the opinion of the commissioners, it is of the utmost importance to the safety and conservation of Boston harbor, that its tidal basins and ways in all the creeks, coves and rivers, above a sectional line, running from Fort Hill to East Boston, should be preserved to the utmost possible extent. If any filling up shall be allowed, an equivalent excavation higher up should be required. No language is strong enough to express the importance of this matter to the interest of the State in the harbor ; and it would be wise for the Legislature to pass an act without delay, prohibiting the diminution of any of the upper tidal basins and ways of Boston harbor, and providing for the payment of such damages as may be just, if any, for taking private property for public uses. And no encroachments whatever upon the tide waters of any part of the harbor, should hereafter be allowed to be made, without notice thereof first being given to the State, or its commissioners, and permission duly obtained therefor.

" The storms are wearing away the headlands and islands, and shoaling the channels in the lower harbor; and the indiscriminate and planless pushing out of shore improvements, is deranging the currents, and filling up the channels and tidal basins of the upper harbor. Hence the natural compensation of causes affecting the conservation of the whole harbor, has become disturbed. The true policy, therefore, in regard to Boston harbor, is a conservative one, to keep it as near as may be, in its structural relations, as nature made it; and it ought never to be subjected to experimental treatment, with a view to make it an artificial harbor, by essentially changing its roadstead, or the form and direction of any of its natural channels.

" All of our existing laws in aid of the harbor, regard and protect it as consisting of two principal elements, to wit : *roadsteads and channels :* and, in the opinion of the commissioners, neither of these essential characteristics should ever be sacrificed, or put in jeopardy, by any land or wharf enterprises upon its shores, to extend beyond the harbor lines already established or recommend-

APPENDIX.   55

ed; and these lines, which have been drawn and fixed at so large an expense to the State, ought never to be disturbed by special legislation or otherwise, for any purpose except a manifest improvement of the harbor."

An act for the extension of the Boston Wharf was again returned to the Senate by Governor Boutwell, together with his objections thereto. By a vote of two-thirds of the Senate, the bill was passed "notwithstanding the said objections," 29th April, 1852.

An act to incorporate the Eastern Avenue Corporation, 1852, chap. 142, was approved by the Governor, April 24th.

The foregoing extracts have been made with care for the purpose of showing, as clearly as possible, the views of the several Boards of Commissioners upon all points of general interest in connection with the harbor.*

---

* It has been, for some years, the custom of the General Court to print all documents of importance that come before them. Subjoined is a list of all the printed documents to be found referring to this subject,—

PRINTED DOCUMENTS OF THE SENATE.

1836.	No. 3*.	Bill to regulate anchorage of vessels in Boston Harbor.
	" 65.	Bill to incorporate the Boston Wharf Company.
1837.	" 47.	Report of Survey of Boston Harbor. See House Doct. No. 63.
1839.	" 30.	Bill to establish regulations concerning Boston Harbor.
1840.	" 8.	Report of Committee to Survey certain parts of Boston Harbor.
	" 37.	Bill concerning Boston Harbor.
1846.	" 8.	Communication from Secretary of War respecting transfer of jurisdiction over certain islands, and act ceding over Governor and Lovell's.
	" 59.	Resolve in relation to Flats
	" 30.	Report and Bill to confirm an act authorizing the Boston Wharf Company to extend their wharves
1847.	" 4.	Message from the Governor, with documents relating to the condition of the islands in Boston Harbor.
	" 25.	Report of Committee on Flats.
	" 58, 78.	Bills to establish regulations for the Harbor of Boston.
	" 63.	Report and resolves relating to Survey of the Harbor.
	" 87.	Report and Bill concerning lines in the same.
	" 97.	Amendment to above bill.
1848.	" 117	Report and Resolve respecting Flats.
	" 134.	Report and Resolve respecting encroachments in the Harbor.
	" 140.	Bill additional to establish regulations concerning Boston Harbor.
1849.	" 50.	Bill ceding to the United States jurisdiction over Great Brewster, &c.
	" 53.	Report of Committee on Survey of Chelsea Creek.
	" 54.	Preliminary Report of Committee on Flats.
	" 119	Report on above report, and Resolve relating to flats in the Harbor.
1850.	" 3.	Report of Commissioners on Flats in Harbor.
	" 119.	Report on above report.
	" 53	Memorial of Roxbury respecting Flats.
	" 115.	Resolve additional authorizing survey of Back Bay.
	" 101.	Bill authorizing extension of wharves in Boston Harbor.
1851.	" 12 .	Report and Resolve giving further time to Commissioners to make final report.
1852.	" 44.	Bill concerning the Boston Wharf Company.
	" 121.	Veto Message on above.
	" 45.	Report of Commissioners on Boston Harbor and Back Bay.
	" 133.	Resolves concerning " " "

APPENDIX.

DECISION OF THE SUPREME JUDICIAL COURT.

The most important of the cases arising under the acts fixing the harbor lines, mentioned in a previous part of this appendix as pending before the Supreme Judicial Court, has since been in effect decided. Pursuant to an order of the Senate, the Clerk of that Board procured a copy of the opinion of the court in that case and caused it to be printed. It is to be found in Senate documents, 1853, No. 109, from which the abstract given below has been made. No final judgment has been given in the case, but the main principles on which it rests are stated very ably and elaborately by the court. The other cases remain under advisement. They are all to a great extent within the principle of the case of the *Commonwealth* vs. *Alger*, though they differ from it in some details of importance to the parties in interest.

SUPREME JUDICIAL COURT.

SUFFOLK COUNTY, March Term, 1853.

Commonwealth vs. *Alger.*

Mr. CHIEF JUSTICE SHAW delivered the opinion of the Court.

After remarking upon the great importance of the case, as affecting the relative rights of the public and of individual proprietors in the soil lying on tide water between high and

PRINTED DOCUMENTS OF THE HOUSE OF REPRESENTATIVES.

1837.	No. 63.	Report and Bill to preserve the Harbor of Boston. See Senate Doc. 47.
1839.	" 65.	Resolves relating to Boston Harbor.
1845.	" 57.	Bill to authorize Boston Wharf Company to extend their wharf.
1846.	" 58.	Memorial of William Appleton and others relating to flats in harbor of Boston.
	" 73.	Statement of Boston Wharf Company relating to the extension of their wharves.
1847.	" 98.	Bill to cede to the U. S. jurisdiction of Minot's Rock in Boston Harbor or Bay.
	" 157.	An Act to establish Regulations concerning Harbor of Boston.
	" 140.	Act to authorize Boston Wharf Company to extend their wharf.
1848.	" 215.	Resolve relating to flats in Harbor of Boston.
1849.	" 59.	Communication from Colonel Thayer, U. S. Engineers, asking cession of Jurisdiction of part of Great Brewster Island.
	" 166.	An Act to preserve that part of Boston Harbor called Chelsea Creek, and to prevent encroachments therein.
1850.	" 74.	Report on Extension of Wharves at East Boston, stating that proprietors of wharves and flats in East Boston have been authorized to extend their wharves t the Commissioner's line established by the act entitled "An Act concerning the Harbor of Boston," passed 17th March, 1840.
	" 141.	An Act in addition to an Act to preserve the Harbor of Boston, and to prevent encroachments therein.
	" 95.	Report of Committee on Mercantile Affairs and Insurance, on petition of Boston Wharf Company.
1851.	" 106.	Report of Commissioners on Boston Harbor and Back Bay.

APPENDIX. 57

low water mark, and stating that the defendant had been indicted at the June term of the Municipal Court in 1849, for having erected a wharf beyond the Commissioners' line, so called, in Boston Harbor, in violation of the Statute, 1847, chapter 278, the learned Chief Justice proceeded to say that the case came up, on the report of the judge of that court who tried it, and that the uncontested facts were these, viz. : The defendant was and had been for more than thirty years the owner of a tract of land, consisting of upland and flats, on or near Fourth Street, in South Boston, bounded on an arm of the sea between South Boston and Boston proper. In 1843 he commenced building a wharf on his said flats, but did not complete it till after the Commissioners' line of 1847 had been established, after which time he built a certain triangular piece of the wharf, which constituted the offence charged in the indictment. This triangular piece was beyond the said Commissioners' line, but on the defendant's own flats, not a hundred rods from the upland, nor below low water mark, and it did no injury to navigation.

The first question then was, what were the right of owners of land bounding on salt water to the flats over which the sea ordinarily ebbs and flows, under the law of Massachusetts ?

In disposing of this question, the rights of owners of flats were deduced primarily from the common law of England and the charters of the colony of Massachusetts, and next from the ordinance of the Colony, passed, probably, in 1647, but commonly termed the ordinance of 1641, relating to the subject. This ordinance, in the opinion of the court, changed the antecedent law which limited the right of private proprietors to ordinary high water mark, and, subsequently to its passage, the grantees of lands bounding on salt water took an estate in fee in the land between high and low water mark, subject to the restriction expressed in the proviso of that ordinance, and to such other limitations of absolute dominion as other real estate is subject to, for the benefit and security of other proprietors and of the public, among which limitations were these ;—that until such lands were enclosed

H

and while they were covered with salt water, all persons had the right to use them for the ordinary purposes of navigation, and that such lands should not be enclosed or built upon so as to impede the public right of way for boats or vessels.

Assuming then that the defendant was the owner in fee of the soil upon which the wharf was built, it remained to inquire whether it was competent for the legislature to pass the acts establishing the lines of the harbor and what was the legal effect of those acts.

It was now clear that the Commonwealth held all the power that existed anywhere, to regulate and dispose of the sea shores and tide waters within its limits and all lands under them, and all public rights connected with them, but this power, however derived, was held in trust for the best interests of the public, and the question was whether the acts under consideration were within the just and legitimate exercise of that power. The object of those acts was to prevent injurious obstructions of the harbor of Boston and to secure the public right of navigation, an object, of course, of deep interest to the public. The principle was well settled that every holder of property in the Commonwealth held it subject to such general regulations as were necessary for the public welfare, and the legislature had the power to subject rights of property, like all other social and conventional rights, to such reasonable restraints and limitations as the common good required. This power was *very different from the right of eminent domain* which authorized the taking of private property for public use, upon condition of making reasonable compensation therefor. It was rather *the police power*—the constitutional power of the legislature to make all manner of wholesome laws for the general good.

It was much easier to perceive the existence of this power than to mark its boundaries. It was exercised without question in the enactment of laws prohibiting the storage of gunpowder, the erection of large wooden buildings, the exercise of noxious trades, or the raising of dams, in particular localities. In cases of this description, though the prohibition might diminish the profits of the owners of the land affected thereby, it did not entitle those owners to compensation. It was *not an appropriation of their property to a public use*, but the restraint of an injurious private use of it by them, and therefore not within the principle of property taken under the right of *eminent domain.*

This distinction, the court thought, was manifest in principle, though the facts and circumstances of different cases were so various, that it was often difficult to decide whether a particular exercise of legislation were properly attributable to the one or the other of these two acknowledged powers. In this connection was cited the case of the *Commonwealth* v. *Tewksbury*, 11 Metcalf's Reports, 55, wherein it was held that the *Stat.* 1845, ch. 117, which imposed a penalty on any person who should remove stones, gravel or sand from certain portions of the beaches of Chelsea, being passed for the protection of the harbor of Boston, extended as well to the owners of the soil as to strangers; and that this was not such a taking of private property for public use as to render the statute unconstitutional, though it provided no compensation to the owners of the land affected by it.*

Some weight was also attached by the court to the consideration that the colonial ordinance which extended the rights of riparian owners to low water mark was not absolute but qualified with the reservation affecting the right of navigation. It was to be presumed that our ancestors, in enacting that ordinance, had in view the rules of the common law, and the practice under them, and that they well understood that all real estate granted by a government to individuals was subject, by reasonable implication, to such restraints in its use as should make its enjoyment by the grantee consistent with the equal enjoyment by others of their several and common rights. When, therefore, in conferring the general right, they reserved some right to individuals and the public of passing with vessels, but without defining that right, it seemed reasonable and just to construe such reservation more liberal-

* By the Stat. 1846, ch. 206, the statute above named was repealed as to part of the beaches owned by Mr. Tewksbury, and $500 were ordered to be paid to him from the treasury " as an indemnity for the loss suffered by him under the operation of said Act, by reason of being unnecessarily debarred from the use of his land, for the purpose, as was intended, of securing the harbor of Boston."

ly in favor of the right reserved than it otherwise would be construed. And it appeared to the court that the legislative power of restraining the injurious use of real estate applied for various reasons more directly to land separating the upland from the sea, than it did to inland property ordinarily used for agricultural purposes. For reasons before given therefore, *the court held that the legislature had the right, in the exercise of the police power before-mentioned, as distinguished from the right of eminent domain, to pass general laws equally affecting all riparian proprietors on the same line of shore, reasonably restraining their use of their property, and sanctioned by suitable penalties.* Wherever there was a general right on the part of the public and a general duty on the part of individuals to respect such right it was competent for the legislature to prescribe a precise rule for declaring and securing it, and the exercise of that power was in most cases where it has occurred, of very great utility. Such cases, for example, were found in the laws regulating the construction and repair of highways and bridges. The court referred, by way of illustration, to several cases establishing the right of the public to have innavigable rivers kept open for the passage of fish to their head waters, and particularly to the case of *Stoughton* v. *Baker*, 4 Mass. Reports, 528, in which it was held that the legislature had the right, in 1835, to require fishways to be made through a dam across the Neponset River, which had been erected in 1633, in pursuance of a grant from the colonial government, which grant contained no reservation providing for the passage of fish. The court referred also, in the same connection, to the provincial act of 15 Geo. II., passed in 1741, by which it was provided that fishways should be constructed, at the expense of the owners, through all dams erected across streams through which certain kinds of fish usually passed, and that the owner of any dam built before 1709 should be reimbursed the first cost of such fishways, but should afterwards maintain them at his own expense. This act was declared to be still in force, in the case of the *Commonwealth* vs. *Chapin*, 5 Pick. Reps. 199. And the court considered that the only ground on which laws of that description could have been made and adjudged valid was, that the right of soil in rivers not navigable was held subject to a public right which might be declared and defined by legislative enactments. In reference to the case before them, the court concluded that it was competent for the legislature to make a law defining the harbor lines, and that it was for the legislature, under a high sense of their duty and responsibility, to make such reasonable regulations as in their judgment were necessary to protect public and private rights. If any portion of the wharf in question had been erected beyond the Commissioners' line before the passage of the act of 1847, then, to such portion that act did not apply. The laws on this subject were all simply prospective in their operation. If indeed, before their passage, any one had so built into navigable water as to cause a nuisance, he might be liable to indictment and punishment, but not under those laws. And any person, who had built on his own soil, before those laws were enacted, in a manner not amounting to a public nuisance at the time of the erection, had only exercised his lawful right; and any law to punish acts lawful at the time they were done would be *ex post facto* and contrary to the constitution and to the plainest principles of justice, and of course void.

In regard to the fact that the wharf built by the defendant did not obstruct navigation, that circumstance afforded no defence. It had been held by the court that the law was valid, and the only question was whether the structure was within or beyond the prohibited limit.

The Chief Justice concluded as follows, viz. :

" On the whole, the court are of opinion that the act fixing a line within the harbor of Boston beyond which no riparian proprietor should erect a wharf or other permanent structure, although to some extent it prohibited him from building such structure on flats of which he owned the fee, was a constitutional law, and one which it was competent for the legislature to make, that it was binding on the defendant, and rendered him obnoxious to its penalties if he violated its provisions."

REMARKS OF LIEUT. C. H. DAVIS.

The following extract from a paper among the Memoirs of the American Academy of Arts and Sciences, written by Lieut. Charles H. Davis, of the U. S. Navy, deserves consideration, Mr. Davis having been employed to execute the hydrographical portion of the survey of Boston Harbor, in connection with the United States Coast Survey, and having been led by his acquaintance with and interest in the subject, as a native of Boston, to make a particular examination of the harbor, " for the purpose of ascertaining what alterations have taken place since the survey of Commodore Wadsworth, in 1817 " He thus closes a series of very interesting scientific remarks,—

" To do justice to our admirable harbor, unsurpassed in its convenience, security and ample dimensions, as it is rarely equalled in its beauty, it may be well to compare it with a few of the principal maritime ports of the world.

" At New York (to begin at home) there are twenty or twenty-one feet of water on the bar, and the mean rise and fall of tides is five feet; the depth at the entrance of the inner harbor of Boston is eighteen feet, and the mean rise and fall of the tides ten feet; making the average depth in the two places about the same. Boston, however, enjoys this double superiority,—that, while at New York the bar is at the outer entrance, and ships must keep the sea until they are able to pass it, at Boston the bar is at the entrance of the inner basin, vessels are landlocked when they reach it, and, if compelled to wait for the tide, can lie in safety; and Boston, moreover, has several excellent roadsteads, in which New York is comparatively deficient.

" At the entrance of the estuary of the Mersey, there are only eleven feet of water at low spring tides; but the rise of tide varies from twenty-one to thirty-one feet. The construction of a new harbor of refuge, at great cost, in this vicinity, is one of the splendid enterprises in which the British are now engaged. The harbors of Dublin are artificial; a bar prevents the entrance of large vessels into the river, and the navigation of the bay is very dangerous in stormy weather. The channel of the river Clyde above Greenwich is only three hundred feet wide, and at Glasgow there is now, after all the remarkably successful improvements made in the navigation of the river, only nine feet of water at low neap tides.

APPENDIX. 63

"Hamburg, the greatest commercial city of Germany, perhaps of the Continent, can only be approached with safety at all times by vessels drawing fourteen feet of water, though vessels drawing eighteen feet can come up with the spring tides. Marseilles, the great emporium of the South of France, the centre of nine-tenths of the commerce of France with the countries bordering on the Mediterranean, has for its port a basin three thousand feet long, and quite narrow, having only sixteen or eighteen feet of water at its entrance, with no perceptible tide, and kept open only by the incessant use of dredging-machines. The port of Havre is kept clear by artificial means.

"But the best idea of the capacity of Boston Harbor, and of the most suitable mode of improving its conveniences for commerce, is obtained by comparing it with London in some particulars; and this comparison is suggested by the report of the commissioners of January, 1850. It is recommended in this report to excavate upon the flats wet docks, in imitation of London and Liverpool, and a plan is submitted in which the place of these docks is drawn, above low-water mark. This recommendation is founded upon a total misconception of the nature of the case, and ignorance of the actual condition of Boston Harbor. Wet docks have been constructed in London at an enormous cost, because they were absolutely indispensable. As the commerce enlarged, the ships that entered the river would have blocked it up, and intercepted all passage, had they not been drawn out on one side or the other. The maintenance of the commercial prosperity of the city depended on having some auxiliary space into which to take vessels that must unavoidably lie still a long time, while discharging, loading, repairing, &c. The natural room was too limited; artificial room was to be created. In the case of Liverpool, docks are required, whatever may be their expense, if a great trade is to be sustained, in consequence of the want of good anchoring-ground in the Mersey, and because it would not under any circumstances be either safe or commodious for vessels to load and discharge cargoes by the side of a pier, or by means of lighters, where the rise and fall of the tide is thirty feet. The cases, therefore, of Boston and London, or Liverpool, are essentially different.

"Neither is it correct to speak of the Atlantic Dock at New York as belonging to the same system as the English docks. The Atlantic Dock is formed by the enclosure of a natural water area, deepened and improved undoubtedly. It is hardly worth while to say, that this is a very distinct thing from the construction of one of the London docks, occupying ground on which formerly stood a populous parish, with its dwellings and churches.

"But while the London docks do not furnish us an example for imitation, we may copy with advantage the plan of the Atlantic

Dock. The water area of the London docks is about one hundred and eighty-eight acres. Now the whole amount of the water area of the Fore Point Channel, including the space between the wharves, added to that of the two Mystic Channels, is about the same as the water area of the London docks. So far, then, from being called upon to excavate wet docks on the South Boston Flats at an incalculable cost, we have merely to inclose these channels suitably, and maintain them in a good state, to have at once a protected water area equal to that of the London docks, but having this remarkable superiority; that by far the greater portion of it is provided with natural reservoirs of back-water, which, if properly treated, will serve always to keep it open. And to all this is still to be added Chelsea Great Creek, the water area of which is in itself equal in amount to that of the London docks, and which, though it has no rear receptacle, possesses in its natural state every advantage of security that art could bestow.

"It is painful to see opinions so erroneous, upon a subject of such vast importance as the preservation of Boston Harbor and the improvement of its commercial accommodations, officially and formally laid before the Legislature of the State.

"If the Fore Point Channel were appropriately walled in, (there being already sufficient wharf-room, and if the proper accessories were provided, there is no reason why it should not, considering its convenience and proximity, take the place in Boston Harbor of the Atlantic Dock in New York. At present it exhibits a melancholy spectacle of resources wasted and opportunities unimproved.

"Regret is sometimes expressed that so large a quantity of the tidal marshes and mudlands should have been filled during the present century. But this operation was the necessary concomitant of the growth of the city, and indeed the very mode of its prosperity and increase. The statesmen and political economists of the day would not have hesitated to sanction and encourage the schemes of aggrandizement of enterprising and sagacious projectors, even if they had foreseen that one of their results would be the loss of water capacity in the main channels of the harbor. Their part was to lay the foundations of our commercial greatness; one of the duties devolved upon us, is to preserve and improve the instruments of commerce; and with prudent measures we shall always have it in our power to secure to Boston Harbor its present reputation of being one of the safest and most commodious in the world."

APPENDIX. 65

COMMUNICATION OF JAMES HAYWARD, ESQ.

Boston, April 18*th*, 1853.

E. H. ELDREDGE, Esq.,—

DEAR SIR :—I have received your note of Saturday, requesting from me " a statement showing that the attention of eminent engineers and of scientific societies in Europe, has, for some years been directed to the subject of tidal harbors and their preservation ; " and, also, that I would give you my " views upon the peculiar wants of our own harbor, and the effect of recently proposed harbor lines."

As to the first of these inquiries, it may be sufficient to say that the subject of the preservation and improvement of harbors has engaged the attention of engineers and governments in Europe, more or less, for many centuries back. For a century back, we have, in considerable detail, the history of tidal rivers and harbors in Great Britain. For that period, these rivers and harbors have been professionally treated, and the results of such treatment recorded for the benefit of those who should come after. Measures for the preservation and improvement of harbors were adopted upon theoretical principles and limited observation at first, and the results of these measures observed and noted. Mistakes were sometimes made :—but even these mistakes form a very important portion of the records of the profession. They serve as beacons to warn others against taking the course in which their predecessors had made shipwreck. By careful observation and cautious experiments, together with minute attention to the modified results of natural agents, produced by artificial appliances,—the science of hydrography has grown up. And it may be safely said that, at the present day, the *principles* of no branch of engineering science are better settled than those of this department of the profession. Occasional discoveries were earlier made ; but it was not till the present century that there was the beginning of any thing like a system with regard to engineering practice in this behalf. There were Smeaton, and Golborne, and Telford, and Nim-

I

mo, and the elder Rennie, who made important contributions to this science; but much has been added more recently. There is probably no one subject which has employed more engineering talent or engineering labor in Great Britain during the present century, than hydrography. Every harbor, even the smallest, has had its resident engineer to look after its welfare. Besides this, for many years, this interest has been the special care of Government. These remarks are true not of Great Britain alone, but of France, Holland, and other European States. We have more details of the history and progress of this subject in Great Britain than elsewhere. A Board of Harbor Commissioners has been established in every port of any importance in the three kingdoms. And, in the 8th of Victoria, a special commission was appointed by the crown, consisting of *ten* gentlemen connected with different branches of the government, who were authorized and directed to make a thorough investigation of the entire subject, and to propose such measures for the preservation and improvement of the harbors, and for the perfecting of the system of supervision and conservation, as they should judge best calculated to promote the object in view. These gentlemen held long sessions; examined engineers and others having knowledge of the condition and wants of the various harbors, and the necessities and conveniences of commerce at the various sea-ports in the kingdom; and then decided on certain regulations to be proposed to government for the better management of these trusts;—and sent to the different harbor boards, circulars containing the proposed regulations, for the purpose of eliciting the opinions of these boards as to the propriety of the changes proposed to be introduced in the management of these important trusts. To give some idea of the magnitude of this system of care for the harbors of Britain, it may be sufficient to state, that the Commissioners received answers to their circular, from about 400 harbor boards.

The examinations of engineers and nautical men before the " Tidal Harbor Commissioners" elicited a vast amount of information; and showed how thoroughly the subject had been studied and how well it was understood. The records of this commission contain a vast number of reports of the most eminent engineers in the country, giving details of their practice and experience on these subjects. These reports are elaborate and able, and they constitute a fund of information for the commercial inquirer, and a treasury of science on this subject for the hydographic engineer. The great success which they have had in preserving and improving tidal rivers by properly directing the currents, is one of the great triumphs of engineering skill. A letter which I received within the last year from the engineer of the harbor of Glasgow, Scotland, gives a striking example of this success. "The size of vessels"—he says—"frequenting this harbor half a century ago, was about 10 or 15 tons; they were open decked fishing boats. Yesterday the H. C. Ridston, 1400 tons register, a sailing ship, left the harbor. To day a steamer of 1800 tons, tomorrow one of 2245 tons register leaves; and two others, each 2400 tons, will in a short time. These are paddle steamers, and do not frequent the Clyde: But it is no unusual thing for ships of 600 or 700 tons to lie at the quays."—Other analogous cases might be cited.

With regard to "the peculiar wants of our own harbor," respecting which you inquire, it is not easy to answer in a few words. The *great* want of Boston harbor,—which includes all the peculiar wants,—is a well devised, intelligent and permanent system of supervision and care. The great danger to the harbor is the piece-meal, irregular and inconsistent legislation which we have in relation to it.

Questions, supposed directly to concern the harbor, are usually sent to the Committee on Mercantile Affairs and Insurance. This Committee is changing every year; it generally consists of gentlemen engaged in trade, who are not supposed to be specially versed in the philosophy of tidal channels and tidal currents. Petitioners for grants lay before that Committee such evidence as they think will establish their own case; probably they are generally honest in their opinion of its propriety; for people usually persuade themselves that what *they* want is reasonable. There being perhaps no private interest opposed to the legislation asked for; and those who see a strong public objection, yet having no responsibility in the case, feel it to be an ungracious act to go up to the legislative hall to state these objections: and the objectionable grant is made. The petitioners for Railroad grants are sent to another Committee, or to two or three other Committees. This is another class of cases which sometimes affect very seriously the interests of navigation. Currents are turned from their proper course; eddies are created; and in a recent instance a very important channel and passageway for vessels has been entirely subverted by a charter from the Legislature of the State. And, even when these Committees are most anxious to avoid mistakes, they have so short a time to inform themselves as to the facts and the deductions to be drawn from them, that they so misapply the general principles of science in these cases, as to put one in mind of an attempt to practice the *healing art* from a book of *recipes* by a man unacquainted with the diagnosis of diseases. The truth is, that every case in hydrography has its peculiar characteristics; and any successful treatment of a case must have reference to all these peculiarities. One is likely to do great mischief by undertaking to prescribe without the requisite skill. Take a single illustration. It is a general rule that, in harbors consisting of river channels,—like Boston harbor,—the necessary *backwater* to scour out these channels should be carefully preserved. This has been so often repeated that there are, in this community, few men who have not a general notion, more or less distinct, of the truth and importance of this axiom. The misfortune is, that there are many people who undertake to play the engineer on these subjects, of whom this axiom constitutes the chief, if not the entire " stock in trade." They are not aware that there may be danger from too much scour as well as from too little. Nor is the *quantity* of scour the only or the principal thing to be cared for in the preservation of a harbor. The *direction* of this reflux current in every part of the channels, and especially in those parts used for navigation, is a most important circumstance. There are other peculiarities in relation to this scouring process, equally important. One single fact further in illustration. A harbor in the south of Europe, which formerly had two rivers emptying their waters into the extreme upper part of that harbor, —somewhat as the Charles and the Mystic empty their waters into Boston Harbor,—was found to be fast filling up. Indeed vast expenditures were required to keep the harbor open, and preserve the proper depth of water for navigation. It was finally decided by the engineers to change entirely the courses of these rivers, so that they should not flow at all into the harbor proper. And their courses were turned in a manner analogous to what would be done here, if Charles river were carried through the low part of Roxbury into Dorchester Bay, and Mystic River were carried, through Chelsea or the back part of East Boston, into the deep water back of Governor's Island. It turned out that the engineers were right in their opinions :—by this change one of the best harbors in Europe was saved probably from entire destruction. But it would be very unsafe to infer from the statement of this case, that this is the proper treatment for every other harbor in which it should be found that *bars* were forming and the channels were becoming less deep. There were peculiar circumstances attending this case, which made the treatment adopted by the engineers the only proper remedy for the evil. And *every* case has its peculiarities and should be treated with a skilful reference thereto. To this end,—and this remark applies with peculiar force to Boston Harbor,—it is not sufficient that there have been careful and ample surveys of the channels and flats, and examinations of the currents; that the characteristics of the former are recorded with sufficient minuteness upon charts, and the latter are indicated in reports. They should be under the supervision and responsible care of an authority which should not be subject to perpetual change; and should be carefully watched and occasionally re-examined, so that no great change can take place without the knowledge of the Board which have the harbor in custody. And when there is a tendency to deterioration the proper preventives should be seasonably used, which will be likely to save the public from the necessity of large expenditures for remedy in the end.

In reply to your inquiry as to my opinion of " the effect of recently proposed harbor lines,"—I must say that I look upon that experiment with the greatest apprehension for the safety of the main channel. The very proposition, to adopt these lines as boundary lines of the harbor, implies that the flats lying between these lines and the shore are to be granted to somebody for the uses of commerce. The next step, therefore, will probably be, to authorize the occupancy of these flats by either solid or pile wharves, as shall be the opinion of the legislature at the time the grant is made. This done and the structures built, it will be found that there is no water (or from 0 to 3 feet) at low-water, at these wharves; and the proprietors of the same, finding their wharves from 1200 to 1500 feet from the navigable channel, will, as a matter of course, ask permission of the legislature to excavate the flats between their property and the main channel; so that they can get their vessels in and out of their docks. This will then be thought a measure of necessity, and will be likely to be granted: and the result of this will be *the ruin of the main channel:* for, as soon as the ground is broken between these lines and that channel, the current at ebb tide, which is very strong in the latter half of the ebb,—and which in consequence of modern structures, sets strongly upon that side of the channel,—will very materially aid this process of excavation, and will sweep this material into the main channel. Thus, from 30 to 60 per cent. would eventually be added to the *width* of this channel, and about the same proportion subtracted from its *depth*.

This widening of the channel, however, would not be likely to proceed with regularity; some parts of the bottom would probably be found to be much harder than other parts; (indeed there is existing evidence of this diversity of character in the flats,) and the channel would, at no very distant day, become essentially injured, if not entirely destroyed. That it would be unsafe to disturb the surface of the flats between the proposed harbor lines and the main channel, there is unmistakable evidence. Since the harbor survey of 1836, many thousand tons of earth have been washed from these flats into the channels by the ordinary operation of the daily tides, in consequence of the surface being broken by the keels of vessels and other accidental causes. How much greater would be the exposure, if, along the margin of the channel, the surface of the flats should be broken up by dredging machines and left to the constant action of the tides, at the place where their power is greatest! There is already an unhealthy action going on in the main channel, occasioned by artificial causes. It is of the greatest importance to the interests of commerce, and therefore to the interests of the City and the State, that nothing should be done to increase this deleterious action; but rather that this work of deterioration should be stayed before we are brought to the necessity of choosing between an immense expense to save the harbor, and an entire destruction of it as a place for large vessels.

It is to be hoped that the South Boston flats, outside the line of private ownership, will not be appropriated till there shall be established, in connexion with their occupancy, a system which,—while it shall add greatly to the commercial conveniences of this port,—shall secure the safety and perfection of the main harbor channel.

There does not seem to be any present necessity for the establishment of harbor lines on that shore. The outer line which is proposed as the limit beyond which no wharves shall ever be built, is more than three-eighths of a mile outside the line of private ownership, more than *three-eighths* of a mile from any improvements for trade on that part of the harbor, and nearly *three-quarters* of a mile from the general line of any such improvements. There is therefore, no occasion for legislative action at present in this behalf: And it is better to wait till a system can be matured which will give the greatest amount of commercial convenience, and at the same time secure the safety of the harbor.

Very respectfully and truly yours,

JAMES HAYWARD.

RESOLUTIONS OF THE CITY COUNCIL.
CITY OF BOSTON.

In Board of Mayor and Aldermen, Nov. 24, 1823.

Resolved, That it is expedient that the Mayor and Aldermen be authorized to cause a geometrical survey of Deer and Rainsford islands to be made, and also of any other islands, whose preservation they shall deem peculiarly important for the safety of the harbor of this City ; also, to cause sufficient stakes or strong monuments to be placed at suitable and measured distances from the present external line of such parts of the bank of said islands, as are exposed to be worn away by the action of the waves or of tempests, and to cause such surveys of the relative position of such stakes or monuments to the bank and to one another to be made, and such plans to be taken and preserved, as may enable the City authorities in any future years to ascertain the nature and degree of loss annually sustained from the elements, on such islands.

Resolved, That it is expedient that a Committee of both branches of the City Council be appointed for the purpose of drafting a respectful memorial to the National Legislature, setting forth the great and successive dilapidation of these islands, their importance to the harbor, and to the shipping, as a barrier and shelter in storms and tempests, and soliciting an efficient appropriation, to be expended, either under the direction of the City authorities, or under such superintendence as the general government may appoint, for their permanent preservation, and that the said memorial, when prepared, be laid before the City Council for consideration and adoption.

Resolved, That it is expedient that the same committee be authorized also to prepare a respectful memorial to the Legislature of this Commonwealth, stating the tenor of the memorial* mentioned in the preceding vote, and praying the countenance and support of the State authorities in behalf o the said application of the City to the General Government, for the objects specified in their said memorial.

Resolved, That the same committee be authorized to apply to the State Legislature for an act, prohibiting under efficient penalties, the removing or carrying away of stones, for ballast or any other purpose from the shores of any of the islands in the harbor, under such restrictions and conditions, as to the wisdom of the Legislature may seem expedient.

Sent down for concurrence. Came up concurred.
Read and concurred.

Boston, March 29, 1852.

A true copy from the records of the City of Boston.

Attest,— SAML. F. McCLEARY, Jr., *City Clerk.*

Vote of the Board of Trustees of the Marine Society.

At a trustee meeting of the Boston Marine Society, held at the Marlboro' Hotel, on Tuesday, the 2d June, 1829, the following communication received from a committee of the City Council, relative to a communication from the Mayor of the City of Boston, on the subject of the flats; it was voted, that Winslow Lewis, Esq. be requested, as a committee, to bring the subject before the Marine Society at their next meeting, (this day) and to obtain their views and opinions as to the expediency of the measures recommended, and to report to an adjourned meeting of the committee of the City Council.

After a deliberate discussion on the subject of the above application, it was unanimously

Voted, That it is the opinion of this Board that a wharf or breakwater, commencing at the dolphin lately put down on the flats opposite the draw on the east side of South Boston Free Bridge, and continued to the end of said flats, opposite to Central wharf, would have the effect of deepening the

J

channel within it, which is daily becoming more shallow to an alarming degree, and would be a means of greatly protecting the wharves in that section from easterly winds, and would add much to the facility of navigation in the harbor of Boston.

A true copy from the record.

Attest,— THOMAS ENGLISH, *Secretary.*

The above is a true copy of a paper accompanying the petition of the City of Boston, and filed with said petition.

Attest,— CHARLES CALHOUN,
Clerk of the Senate.

Extract from a letter from Gen. Totten, of the Engineers' Department, to Hon. William Appleton, in answer to inquiries made at the request of the Committee, as to the appropriations by Congress for the construction of the sea wall upon the Great Brewster Island, and the amount necessary to complete the work.

"In compliance with the further desire of the Department, Col. Thayer made an estimate of the amount necessary to complete the work, over and above the sum already applicable; which estimates was submitted to Congress by the Secretary of War, with the estimates for Rivers and Harbors on the Atlantic, the amount being - - - $32,700.00

The first appropriation for this work, July 20, 1848,	$40,000.00
The next, and last, August 30, 1852, - - -	30,000.00

"Wanted to complete, according to the estimates of Col. Thayer, $32,700, provided the work can go on continuously,—excepting from the interruption of winter,—and this may be the case, if the requisite grant is made early in the next session. If there is another suspension of operations, the cost will be magnified materially."

Dated Engineer Department, Washington, March 17, 1853.

APPENDIX. 75

The following table showing the comparative size of the vessels registered in this District, together with the accompanying list, were prepared by General Andrews of the Registry Office, Boston Custom House.

Vessels Measured at Boston.

Years Meas'd.	No. Vessels.	Denomination.	Tonnage.	Av. Tonnage.	Total.
1800	9	Ships,	2,247	250	2,247
	No barks measured this year.				
1844	16	Ships,	8,365	523	
	16	Barks,	4,624	289	12,989
1845	15	Ships,	8,380	558	
	16	Barks,	4,317	269	12,697
1849	20	Ships,	14,162	708	
	16	Barks,	4,416	276	18,578
1850	23	Ships,	21,291	926	
	12	Barks,	4,392	366	25,683
1851	27	Ships,	27,535	1,019	
	11	Barks,	3,430	311	30,965
1852	35	Ships,	35,057	1,001	
	4	Barks,	1,278	319	36,335
From Jan. 1 to Oct. 1, '53,	35	Ships,	43,257	1,236	
	5	Barks,	1,563	313	44,820

Tonnage of Ships and Barks registered at the Boston Custom House.

Date.	Name of Vessels.	Tons.	Date.	Name of Vessels.	Tons.
	1850.		Aug.	16, Bark Ella,	196
January 9,	Ship William Sturgis,	650		21, Ship Gentoo,	747
10,	" Clara Wheeler,	996	Sept.	3, " Shirley,	911
10,	" Tirrell,	943		24, " John Bryant,	722
April 18,	" Moses Wheeler,	872		24, Bark Geo. E. Webster,	˙354
May 3,	" Greenwich,	787		28, Ship Antarctic,	1116
4,	Bark Rhone,	360		28, " John H. Jarvis,	741
13,	" Wabash,	299	Oct.	9, " Prospero,	646
14,	Ship Hemisphere,	949		15, " Surprise,	1262
21,	" Trimountain,	1032		25, " Union,	688
June 8,	" Sachem,	718		28, Bark Sumpter,	381
15,	" Cornelius Grinell,	1118	Nov.	12, Ship Art Union,	750
19,	Bark Kremlin,	470		16, Bark Behring,	376
26,	" May Queen,	325		18, " Paragon,	309
July 6,	" Sultana,	452		22, Ship Meridian,	1285
30,	" Race Horse,	514	Dec.	5, " Daniel Webster,	1188
Aug. 2,	" Isabella,	356		21, " Stag Hound,	1534
6,	Ship President,	1021			
16,	" Berkshire,	615			25,683

APPENDIX.

Date.	Name of Vessels.	Tons.	Date.	Name of Vessels.	Tons.
1851.			Sept. 6,	Ship Malay,	868
Jan'ry 16,	Ship Witchcraft,	1310	17,	" Gem of the Ocean,	702
16,	" John Bertram,	1081	28,	" John Gilpin,	1089
21,	" Gamecock,	1392	Oct. 5,	" Agnes,	929
March 7,	" Hamlet,	757	11,	" Westward Ho,	1650
7,	Bark Kedar,	347	27,	" Queen of the Seas,	1356
15,	" Ala,	464	Nov. 6,	" Whirlwind,	961
17,	Ship Shooting Star,	903	10,	" Alexander,	596
22,	" Napoleon,	649	12,	" Lotus,	660
27,	" Andes,	450	12,	" Winged Racer,	1767
April 9,	Bark Edisto,	366	22,	" Bald Eagle,	1704
26,	Ship Flying Cloud,	1782	29,	" Golden Eagle,	1121
May 1,	Bark Mermaid,	533	Dec. 4,	" National Eagle,	1049
1,	Ship Southern Cross,	938	9,	" Golden West,	1441
8,	" Telegraph,	1069	14,	" Flying Childers,	1126
12,	Bark Echo,	196	20,	" Star of the Union,	1057
30,	Ship Syrene,	1064	21,	" Hussar,	721
30,	" Courser,	1025	24,	Bark Richmond,	199
July 8,	Bark Chester,	200	31,	Ship Phantom,	1289
Aug. 1,	Ship Staffordshire,	1817			
6,	Bark J. H. Duvall,	200		Total,	36,335
20,	Ship John Wade,	639		1853.	
20,	" R. B. Forbes,	756	Jan'y 13,	Ship Mountain Wave,	633
29,	" Coringa,	701	28,	" Emp'ss of the Sea,	2197
29,	" Sam'l Lawrence,	1035	28,	" Golden Light,	1141
29,	Bark Georgiana,	195	31,	" Champion,	1023
29,	Ship Caroline,	722	Feb'ry 1,	" Radiant,	1318
Oct. 13,	" Robert Harding,	765	1,	" Mystery,	1155
13,	" North America,	1464	March 5,	" Storm King,	1289
20,	" Susan Hincks,	783	18,	" Climax,	1051
Nov. 5,	" Flying Fish,	1505	24,	" Competitor,	1871
12,	" Geo. Washington,	1534	April 1,	" Queen of Clippers,	2361
15,	" Northern Light,	1021	1,	" Star of Empire,	2050
19,	Bark Modena,	200	1,	" Cleopatra,	1563
Dec. 5,	" Sea Bird,	334	1,	Bark Firefly,	401
6,	Ship Antelope,	507	18,	Ship John Land,	1065
13,	Bark Rocket,	395	May 5,	" Wizard,	1601
Dec. 30,	Ship Hoogly,	1304	10,	Bark Wildfire,	338
31,	St'mship Rajah Wallie,	562	10,	Ship West Wind,	1071
			20,	" White Swallow,	1192
		30,965	24,	" Shawmut,	1035
	1852.		25,	" Waverley,	750
Jan'y 27,	Ship Dauntless,	791	26,	" Water Witch,	1204
Feb'ry 4,	" Ocean Eagle,	597	June 3,	" Chariot of Fame,	2500
5,	" Polar Star,	667	14,	" Wild Ranger,	1045
May 4,	Bark Old Hickory,	432	15,	" Bronita,	1127
6,	Ship Beverly,	676	17,	Bark Daniel Webster,	264
8,	" Lady Franklin,	464	July 5,	Ship Whistler,	942
27,	" Lanark,	299	6,	" Amphritrite,	1686
28,	" Ellen Foster,	997	26,	Bark Young Turk,	343
June 16,	" Cape Cod,	774	22,	Ship Edith Rose,	510
19,	" Sov'n of the Seas,	2421	30,	Bark Tally Ho,	217
19,	" Stephen Glover,	733	Aug. 25,	Ship Fearless,	1184
24,	Steamship Sir J. Harvey,	620	30,	" Matchless,	1033
25,	" City of Boston,	559	Sept. 1,	" Lightfoot,	1996
July 1,	Bark Thorndike,	399	9,	" Ocean Pearl,	847
16,	Ship Polynesia,	1084	19,	" Sea Flower,	1024
27,	" Onward,	874	28,	" King Fisher,	1286
August 2,	" Winged Arrow,	1052	30,	" Neptune,	1033
10,	" Golden Fleece,	968	Oct. 1,	" Reporter,	1474
13,	Bark Celistia,	248			
17,	Ship Celestial Empire,	1395		Total,	44,820

APPENDIX. 77

E. H. ELDREDGE, Esq.

Dear Sir : In reply to your letter requesting information from the Pilots of Boston, in reference to the changes that have taken place in the Channels, and the state of the Islands in the lower harbor, my opinion is based upon an experience of forty-five years, the changes in that term of years have proved detrimental, and they will continue to increase unless those changes are met with the interest that a subject of so much importance demands. The Islands and headlands have been constantly wasting away, and of course washing their waste matter into the Channels, thereby creating and adding to the *shoal bottom.* The Great Brewster, which is now partially protected by a Sea Wall, has been too much neglected; it should be finished with all the despatch that can be practically applied, if not, the wasting away of that Island will prove the ruin of our harbor, but if properly fortified with a piece of masonry, such as it requires, succeeding generations will appreciate it as a valuable legacy, for it will be the main protector of our harbor and channels, and the basis on which we must depend for the future increase of our commercial interests.

There are other points that claim the consideration of all who are interested in this subject, viz : The Narrows — the main ship channel — removing the top surface from the beaches bordering on the Narrows is injurious, and has proved itself so, especially from the beach of Gallop's Island, as the south gales sweep across it and wash the loose matter into the channel. The southeast and northwest points of Lovell's Island have made and are making out into the Narrows; — also the northwest point of the Spit, which, if not arrested from further progress, will be the cause of material injury.

To prevent further encroachment in the Narrows, it is the opinion of all, who are practically informed, that a breakwater built across Black Rock from Lovell's Island to the Spit would be a sure protection to that channel, as it would turn the force of the rapid cross-current natural to Black

Rock, and create a regular current in the Narrows; the various currents running into the Narrows have caused eddies, and the extension of the points, which if allowed to increase, will in time entirely obstruct that passage.

Other material improvements might be made in the harbor, that would create a confidence in all who have to navigate it. Barrel Rock in Broad Sound should be removed, and large prominent beacons and buoys placed in proper positions. Such valuable acquisitions should not be out of place to act as decoys, but rather as guides, that all who are dependent upon them may have an implicit reliance that they are truly positioned. Such is not the case with many of the beacons recently built. The inner harbor should also receive some notice; much good may arise through the introduction of more prominent buoys, *located properly;* and dredging away the upper middle would improve the capacity of our harbor in that vicinity. I would also suggest to you the propriety of erecting landmarks upon the Graves, Outer Brewster and Egg Rock, so they may be distinguished from each other when made in thick weather, and there should be a beacon erected upon the Harding's Rocks, which are so much dreaded by all approaching the Harbor in thick weather.

My opinion is, that all of the headlands that are openly exposed to the force of the easterly gales should be protected by sea-walls.

I do not suggest these few ideas with any selfish interest, either personal or professional, but for the general good, as it is daily demonstrated in the perseverance of the merchants, the increase of commercial business, as well as the enormous increase in the tonnage of ships, that the public should turn their attention to the preservation of our fine harbor, without which Boston would be a mere cypher in the catalogue of commercial cities.

I am respectfully yours, &c.

HENRY GURNEY.

APPENDIX. 79

Extract from the Report of the Light House Board, to the Secretary of the Treasury, dated January 30, 1853.

BOSTON LIGHT.

Revolving sea-coast and harbor light. William Long, principal and only keeper — was a sea captain. Fourteen 21-inch English parabolic reflectors; lamps and burners American. Plating and reflectors good — scratched in cleaning. Depth of reflector $8\frac{3}{4}$ inches; $6\frac{1}{2}$ inches for ordinate; placed on two faces only. Lantern, iron. Plate-glass, 24x36 inches. Ventilators good — circular — resembling furnace registers. Lantern too small for present arrangement of the lamps and reflectors; keeper absent. Dome of lantern and inside sashes, if not black, not very clean. Iron floor and iron staircase. Tower of rough-hammered masonry, laid in courses with lime-mortar, well pointed. Arch to lantern floor of brick; dry inside; six iron bands around the tower outside. Tower wants whitewashing inside and out, and a little painting. Two copper conductors — one broken and neglected by the keeper; all the bands of the tower touching the conductors. Tower cracked. Fog-bell moved by machinery; weights or hammers too light. Keeper took charge October 20, 1849. Does not light up at sunset, and puts out before sunrise. Has a cistern for rain water. Cellar for oil under dwelling not in order. Oil-tanks want painting. No curtain to protect the apparatus. Dwelling-house in good order and clean. *Buoys in the harbor and its approaches too small; generally spar-buoys, and small of their kind.*

Printed in Dunstable, United Kingdom